Analytical Grammar

Level 2
Mechanics
Instructor Handbook

Created by R. Robin Finley

ANALYTICAL GRAMMAR.

888-854-6284
analyticalgrammar.com
customerservice@demmelearning.com

Analytical Grammar: Level 2, Mechanics Instructor Handbook
© 1996 R. Robin Finley
© 2022 Demme Learning, Inc.
Published and distributed by Demme Learning

All rights reserved. No part of this book may be reproduced, stored in a retrieval system, or transmitted in any form by any means—electronic, mechanical, photocopying, recording, or otherwise—without prior written permission from Demme Learning.

analyticalgrammar.com

1-888-854-6284 or 1-717-283-1448 | demmelearning.com
Lancaster, Pennsylvania USA

ISBN 978-1-60826-656-2
Revision Code 1122

Printed in the United States of America by CJK Group
  2 3 4 5 6 7 8 9 10

For information regarding CPSIA on this printed material call: 1-888-854-6284 and provide reference # 1122-11012022

Table of Contents

Get Started with Analytical Grammar
Welcome to Analytical Grammar vii
Getting Started... viii
Potential Activities xi
Tips for Success xi

Lesson-to-Lesson Instructions
Lesson 1: Comma Splits 1
Lesson 2: Commas—Items in a Series 7
Lesson 3: Commas—Two Adjectives Tests 15
Lesson 4: Commas—Compound Sentences 25
Lesson 5: Commas—Introductory Elements.......................... 35
Lesson 6: Commas—Interrupters................................... 45
Lesson 7: Commas—Names, Dates, & Places 57
Lesson 8: Direct Quotations.. 67
Lesson 9: Titles... 79
Lesson 10: Possessives... 89
Lesson 11: Capitalization 101
Lesson 12: Pronoun-Antecedent Agreement........................ 113
Lesson 13: Subject-Verb Agreement 125
Lesson 14: Which Pronoun? 137
Lesson 15: Adjective or Adverb?................................... 149
Lesson 16: Transitive and Intransitive Verbs....................... 161

Bibliography **173**

Level 2 | Mechanics

Level 2: Mechanics

Welcome to Analytical Grammar!

Children begin learning the grammar of their native language long before they can speak it fluently. Even a toddler knows that "Dad ate pizza" makes sense, while "Pizza ate dad" is silly! Unlike other subjects, we already know the grammar of our daily language—even if we don't know that we know it. The key, therefore, is two-fold:

- Apply labels to the different parts of speech and grammar. We know grammar; we just may not know the names of things or why they are organized in certain ways.

- Understand how to use different language and grammar in different situations. While formal situations call for more formal language, the grammar of our everyday, informal language is not incorrect. Correct grammar changes depending on the situation. Just as a person using informal slang might be judged in a formal setting, the opposite is true: using formal language in an environment where casual language is the norm would seem strange.

These two components combine to make us better writers and, therefore, better communicators. Consistent use of grammar and proper use of punctuation helps keep written information flowing easily to the reader. With a mature understanding of grammar, students are better able to share their increasingly complex thoughts and ideas in a clear, understandable way.

Getting Started

Some grammar "rules" are unbreakable. A sentence must always have a subject and a verb, for example. However, in many cases, rather than "rules," they should be looked at as "guidelines." Even professional grammarians (We do exist!) disagree on things like what a prepositional phrase is modifying in a sentence. Sometimes we even disagree with ourselves from day to day! This is okay. A sentence can be grammatically correct even if there is disagreement about how it is parsed or diagrammed. If your student has enough grammar knowledge to make an informed argument as to why they believe a certain answer is correct, it's a win—give them credit and move on.

The goal of each lesson is that students acquire enough familiarity with the topic that they can achieve 80% on the assessment. *Analytical Grammar* is intended to be an open-book curriculum, meaning that students are encouraged to use the lesson notes to complete all exercises and assessments, so this should not be a difficult goal if students are completing the exercises. Also, once introduced, concepts are repeated in each lesson, so perfect mastery is not required before moving on.

Grammar is a cumulative process. While new topics will be addressed in subsequent lessons, students will continue to practice what they have already learned, and new skills will build upon that knowledge.

Analytical Grammar is just one component of a complete language arts program, which should include literature, writing, and vocabulary or spelling. By dividing the program into five levels, students are able to spend a short time of their school year focusing on grammar, then concentrate more fully on another component armed with the skills to improve their communication.

Components

Analytical Grammar is separated into five levels

Level 1: Grammar Basics: elementary introduction to the nine parts of speech
Level 2: Mechanics: elementary guidelines for punctuation and word usage
Level 3: Parts of Speech: complex information about parts of speech and their interactions
Level 4: Phrases and Clauses: advanced work with more complex components
Level 5: Punctuation and Usage: in-depth information about punctuation and word usage

For each level, you will need these components:

Student Worktext

- *Student Notes* provide instruction and examples for each topic
- *Exercises A, B, & C* give students plenty of practice in applying their new knowledge
- *Assessments* are always open book and provide an accurate measure of proficiency

Instructor's Handbook

- Page-by-page Student Worktext copy with solutions for all student work
- Instructor tips with additional explanation on possible points of confusion
- Item-by-item scoring guide for all assessments

INSTRUCTOR NOTES

16-Week Schedule

The study of grammar is just one part of a complete language arts program. Your student is expected to progress through the Analytical Grammar lessons at their own pace, then continue to practice grammar skills while studying another area of Language Arts.

Lessons

Week 1	Lesson 1
Week 2	Lesson 2
Week 3	Lesson 3
Week 4	Lesson 4
Week 5	Lesson 5
Week 6	Lesson 6
Week 7	Lesson 7
Week 8	Lesson 8
Week 9	Lesson 9
Week 10	Lesson 10
Week 11	Lesson 11
Week 12	Lesson 12
Week 13	Lesson 13
Week 14	Lesson 14
Week 15	Lesson 15
Week 16	Lesson 16

INSTRUCTOR NOTES

An *Analytical Grammar* Week
Most *Analytical Grammar* lessons are set up in the same manner: a page of notes, three exercises, and an assessment. The following is a suggested schedule for completing one lesson a week.

Monday

Read over the lesson notes with your student.

Have your student **complete Exercise A.**

- Work the first one or two sentences together, then have your student complete the rest.
- Remind them that they can use the lesson notes as needed throughout the week.
- Encourage them to ask for as much help as they need.

Tuesday

Review Exercise A.

- This should take no more than 20 minutes.

Have your student **complete Exercise B.**

Wednesday

Review Exercise B.

Have your student **complete Exercise C.**

Thursday

Review Exercise C.

Friday

Have your student **complete the assessment.**

- Remind them that it is open book and they should use the lesson notes as much as necessary.

The following Monday

Correct the assessment together.

- You read out the answers as your student crosses out any incorrect answers.
- Then, using the scoring guide found in the Instructor's Handbook on the assessment key, total up the correct answers and record the score on the test.

Now, **introduce the next lesson** and start the process all over again!

Potential Activities

Short Answers and Fill-in-the-Blanks
Some exercises include short answer and fill-in-the-blank questions. These include activities like providing definitions, identifying a word's job in a sentence, and revising sentences to have proper punctuation.

Editing
As part of many exercises, students will edit a short paragraph. Using editing symbols, they apply their new learning and review their prior learning in a practical situation.

Assessment
On the fifth day of a lesson, students have an opportunity to show you and themselves what they have learned. They will be asked to complete exercises that are similar to the daily exercises. Points are assigned to each section; they are found in the Instructor's Handbook with the solutions. The points are intended to be a measuring stick for how confident the student feels about the material. Remember, your student can use their lesson notes to complete the assessment. They should not try to complete it from memory, without support. Before moving to the next lesson, the goal is for your student to receive at least 80% on the assessment. If your student scores less than 80%, we recommend you review that lesson's notes with them before introducing the next topic and provide heavier support as they begin the new lesson's exercises.

Tips for success
This course can be adapted to meet your student's needs.

- If a lesson feels overwhelming and your student needs to slow down a little, have them do the odd sentences in an exercise one day and the evens the next.

- Remind your student that they can look at the lesson notes for help as they are completing the exercises and even the assessment.

Lesson 1
Comma Splits

Lesson 1: Comma Splits

The first important punctuation mark you're going to learn about is the **comma**. It's just a little thing, but it makes a big difference when it's used properly (or when it isn't). Commas tell the reader when to pause while they're reading and are used to divide sentences into more understandable pieces. Commas are essential!

Example: I like peanut butter and jelly and my mom and dad enjoy bacon lettuce and tomato.

Did it take you a couple of tries to figure out what that sentence means? Now, try it with commas:

I like peanut butter and jelly, and my mom and dad enjoy bacon, lettuce, and tomato.

Ahhh, it's so much easier to read!

There are rules about where commas should go, but, just as importantly, there are also rules about where they should **not** go! We're going to start with those first.

Comma splits

A **comma split** is when you put a comma where it doesn't belong and incorrectly divide a sentence. It is a single comma that comes between two words, phrases, or clauses that shouldn't be separated. Just as commas in the right places make sentences easier to read, commas in the wrong places can be confusing and cause your reader to lose track of what you're trying to communicate. There are six places where a comma never belongs:

1) There should never be **only one** comma between a **subject** and a **verb**.
   Example: The dog, walked into the garage.

2) There should never be **only one** comma between a **verb** and its **direct object**.
   Example: The man threw, the ball.

3) There should never be **only one** comma between a **linking verb** and a **complement** (predicate nominative or predicate adjective).
   Example: The girl felt, wonderful! *or* That girl is, my sister.

4) There should never be **only one** comma between an **adjective** and a **noun** (if there are several adjectives, the one right before the noun).
   Example: The fluffy, sweater was beautiful.

5) There should never be **only one** comma between a **verb** and its **indirect object**.
   Example: I wrote, my aunt a letter.

6) There should never be **only one** comma between an **indirect object** and its **direct object**.
   Example: I wrote my aunt, a letter.

The next few lessons are about comma rules; you'll need to refer to these notes about comma splits to help answer the questions. It's important to take some time to really understand them.

Remember the Six Deadly Comma Splits!

1) subject and verb
2) action verb and direct object
3) linking verb and complement
4) adjective and noun
5) action verb and indirect object
6) indirect object and direct object

Parse the sentence first to help you identify whether there's a deadly split!

Comma Splits: Exercise A

Directions

Each of the following sentences includes one of the Six Deadly Comma Splits. Find and circle the comma. Then write what is being split. Look at the lesson notes if you need help. You might find it helpful to parse the sentence first. The first one has been done for you as an example.

Example: The giant, spider crawled up the back of my chair.

splits adjective (giant) and noun (spider)

1) The catcher, threw the ball back to the pitcher.

   splits subject (catcher) and verb (threw)

2) My favorite dessert is, ice cream.

   splits linking verb (is) and complement (ice cream)

3) Dad brought Jenna, her lunch.

   splits indirect object (Jenna) and direct object (lunch)

4) Jorge runs, the booster club at school.

   splits verb (runs) and direct object (club)

5) The sun, peeked out from behind the clouds.

   splits subject (sun) and verb (peeked)

1 EXERCISE B

Comma Splits: Exercise B

Directions
Each of the following sentences includes one of the Six Deadly Comma Splits. Find and circle the comma. Then write what is being split (parse the sentence if you need to). Remember to look at the lesson notes if you need help.

1) The chair, broke as I tried to sit on it.

   splits subject (chair) *and verb* (broke)

2) Javy's new bicycle is, red.

   splits linking verb (is) *and complement* (red)

3) All of the holiday, decorations must be taken down by Saturday.

   splits adjective (holiday) *and noun* (decorations)

4) I checked, my email before going home.

   splits verb (checked) *and direct object* (email)

5) I handed, the conductor my ticket.

   splits verb (handed) *and indirect object* (conductor)

Comma Splits: Exercise C

Directions

Each of the following sentences includes one of the Six Deadly Comma Splits. Find and circle the comma that is in the wrong place. Then write what is being split (parse the sentence if you need to). Remember to look at the lesson notes if you need help.

1) The big, brown⊙ bear ran across the road.

    splits adjective (brown) *and noun* (bear)

2) My aunt brought me⊙ a gift from Bulgaria.

    splits indirect object (me) *and direct object* (gift)

3) I cleaned⊙ the mirror with vinegar and water.

    splits verb (cleaned) *and direct object* (mirror)

4) She⊙ drove her new car home.

    splits subject (She) *and verb* (drove)

5) My brother and I gave⊙ Mom a plant for Mother's Day.

    splits verb (gave) *and indirect object* (Mom)

1 EXERCISE D

Comma Splits: Exercise D

Directions
Instead of an assessment for this lesson, we've included an extra exercise to practice finding comma splits. In each sentence, find and circle the comma that is in the wrong place. Then write what is being split (parse the sentence if you need to). Remember to look at the lesson notes if you need help.

1) The drinking, glass shattered on the tile floor.

   splits adjective (drinking) *and noun* (glass)

2) My dog's name is, Rufus.

   splits linking verb (is) *and complement* (Rufus)

3) The cat's purrs, made a soothing vibration.

   splits subject (purrs) *and verb* (made)

4) I am growing, tomatoes in my garden this year.

   splits verb (am growing) *and direct object* (tomatoes)

5) The store offered me, a replacement for the damaged item.

   splits indirect object (me) *and direct object* (replacement)

Lesson 2
Commas—Items in a Series

Lesson 2: Commas—Items in a Series

Each of our comma rules will have a "buzzword" that we'll use when we talk about it. The first rule's buzzword is **items in a series**.

Items in a series

Use commas between items in a list or series. These can be individual words or prepositional phrases, but the list always needs to be made of grammatical equals: all nouns, all verbs, all prepositional phrases, and so on. Put a comma between each item and also one before the conjunction that comes before the last item.

Here are just a few examples—there are many more ways to list things.

Examples:

Nouns: I brought my ball, bat, mitt, and hat to the baseball game.

Verbs: I walked, ran, hopped, and jumped to get my exercise today.

Adjectives: She was tall, glamorous, and beautiful.

Prepositional phrases: We looked in the kitchen, under the dining room table, and on top of the fridge for my sister's artwork.

Nouns with prepositional phrases as modifiers: My chore list says to put the dishes into the dishwasher, the glasses into the cabinet, and the silverware into the drawer.

Verbs with prepositional phrases as modifiers: Little Red Riding Hood walked through the woods, skipped down the path, and knocked on her grandmother's door.

> **Note:** If the items in the list are separated by *and* or *or*, don't use commas to separate them.
>
> **Example:** I bought a teddy bear and a necklace and a new shirt.

The comma before the conjunction is called the *serial* comma, or sometimes the Oxford comma. It's named after the University of Oxford in Oxford, England, which is the oldest university in the English-speaking world. Some people say that this comma can be left out. Not us! People can get confused when it's left out, so we think it should always be included.

Example: On my desk, I have pictures of my parents, Spot and Whiskers.

Are you giggling? This sentence makes it seem like Spot and Whiskers are my parents! Let's try it with the serial comma:

On my desk, I have pictures of my parents, Spot, and Whiskers.

Now it's clear: there are three separate pictures! That's better. No one will be confused if you include the serial comma, but people could be if you leave it out. That's why you should always use it.

> **Here's a trick:** If you read any of the sentences out loud, just the way you would say them in real life, your voice will pause right where the commas go. So, in the following exercises, if you have to put commas in a sentence where we've left the commas out on purpose, try reading it out loud, and your voice will tell you where the commas go! This isn't a replacement for understanding the comma rules, but it's a great starting point.

Throughout this book, you will have exercises in **editing**. **Editing** is preparing written text for publishing, or to be read by others. When you **edit**, you correct any mistakes you find in sentences. You might add something that is missing, remove something that shouldn't be there, or change something that is incorrect.

There are certain symbols that we use when editing. You will use these symbols in the editing activities in each lesson.

Here are your first two symbols:

To insert a comma (or anything else): ∧

    red∧ white, and blue

To remove a comma (or anything else): ⁄

    remove ~~this~~

2 EXERCISE A

Commas—Items in a Series: Exercise A

Directions
In each sentence, insert commas where they should go. Look at the lesson notes if you need help.

1) My brother, mother, sister, and I went on a trip to the mall.

2) We had to find shoes for my brother, a hat for my sister, and a new skirt for me.

3) My brother found some sneakers that were red, white, and black.

4) I yelled, jumped, and waved to get Mom's attention.

5) Mom had to walk through the racks, around a display, and over to the corner to get to me.

6) I found a perfect skirt made of denim, cotton, and eyelet lace.

Directions
Edit the errors in the following sentences. There are five errors. Use the editing marks shown in the lesson notes.

7) I asked⌿ Mom if I could buy the skirt. I needed, wanted, and desired that skirt! Mom looked at the beautiful⌿ skirt on the hanger and told me to try it on. I went into the dressing room, closed the door, and tried on the skirt.

Commas—Items in a Series: Exercise B

Directions
In each sentence, insert commas where they should go. Look at the lesson notes if you need help.

1) The skirt was twirly, swirly, and fun!

2) Mom said we could buy the skirt, go back into the mall, and look for a hat for my sister.

3) We went to the checkout counter, paid for the skirt, and got our change.

4) We looked, searched, and finally discovered a hat store.

5) My sister needed a hat that she could wear for the beach, the pool, and the back yard.

Directions
Edit the errors in the following sentences. There are five errors. Use the editing marks shown in the lesson notes. (Remember to look for the Six Deadly Comma Splits, too!)

6) It's always, a good idea to wear a hat when you're out in the sun. The hat can be made of straw, or cotton, or polyester. What is important is that it protects you from the sun's UVA rays, UVB rays and heat. Protect, your face from the sun!

2 EXERCISE C

Commas—Items in a Series: Exercise C

Directions
In each sentence, insert commas where they should go. Look at the lesson notes if you need help.

1) My sister walked into the hat store, down the aisle, and up to the counter.

2) She asked the salesperson which hat would be best for the beach, the back yard, and the pool.

3) The salesperson was helpful, cheerful, and knowledgeable.

4) We watched the salesperson circle the store, select hats, and help my sister.

5) My sister was happy with her new hat for the beach, pool, and back yard.

Directions
Edit the errors in the following sentences. There are five errors. Use the editing marks shown in the lesson notes. (Remember to look for the Six Deadly Comma Splits, too!)

6) By this time, Mom was tired of~~,~~ walking around the mall spending money. My sister, brother, and I told her how much we appreciated the shopping trip. Mom~~,~~ smiled and said she was happy to take us. We kids were proud that we were well behaved, appreciative, and fun.

ASSESSMENT 2

Commas—Items in a Series: Assessment

Directions

In each sentence, insert commas where they should go. Look at the lesson notes if you need help.

Each correctly placed comma is worth one point.

__2__ 1) It was time to head to the food court and eat, talk, and relax!

__2__ 2) Mom and my sister wanted pizza, my brother wanted chicken tenders, and I wanted a burrito bowl.

__2__ 3) The pizza was covered in pepperoni, mushrooms, and extra cheese.

__2__ 4) My brother's system for dipping chicken tenders was to use ketchup, barbecue sauce, and honey mustard.

__2__ 5) My burrito bowl was artfully created with cheese on the left, salsa on the right, and refried beans in the middle.

__10__
10

Directions

Edit the errors in the following sentences. There are five errors. Use the editing marks shown in the lesson notes. (Remember to look for the Six Deadly Comma Splits, too!) Look at the lesson notes if you need help.

Each corrected error is worth one point, for five total points.

6) It was, time to head home after we ate. We pulled, dragged, and pushed our purchases to the car. Thank goodness there, was room in the trunk for it all! My mom, sister, brother, and I talked all the way home. We had, a great time going to the mall as a family.

__5__
5

__15__ Total Points $\frac{12}{15} = 80\%$ 100%
15

Lesson 3
Commas—Two Adjectives Tests

Instructor Notes

This lesson can be difficult for some students. Be generous when reviewing their work, and be ready to talk about why answers might be considered "right" or "wrong."

Lesson 3: Commas—Two Adjectives Tests

The buzzword for this rule is **two adjectives tests**.

A comma should *sometimes* be used between two or more adjectives that come before a noun. It's that *sometimes* that makes us nervous. How are we supposed to know when we need a comma and when we don't? Don't worry—there are a couple of tests you can do to check!

1) **"And" test**

   If it sounds natural to put the word **and** between the adjectives, you need a comma. If adding **and** makes the sentence read less smoothly, leave the comma out.

   Example 1: That is a lovely soft fuzzy sweater.

   Test: *a lovely **and** soft sweater*   Sounds good. We need a comma.

   *a soft **and** fuzzy sweater*   Sounds good. We need a comma.

   The sentence needs two commas:

   That is a lovely, soft, fuzzy sweater.

   Example 2: I saw a little old man.

   Test: *a little **and** old man*   Sounds odd. Forget the comma.

   The sentence is correct without commas:

   I saw a little old man.

2) **Order test**

   Try changing the order of the adjectives. If it still sounds right without changing the meaning, you need commas. Let's use the same example sentences as above to check this test:

   Example 1: That is a lovely soft fuzzy sweater.

   Test: *a soft lovely fuzzy sweater*   Sounds good.

   a fuzzy soft lovely sweater   Sounds good.

   a lovely fuzzy soft sweater   Sounds good.

   Yes, these all sound just fine, as does any other combination we could come up with. We need commas between the adjectives:

   That is a lovely, soft, fuzzy sweater.

   Example 2: I saw a little old man.

   Test: *an old little man*   Sounds odd (to native English speakers)

   No, we shouldn't change the order, because it makes the reader stumble over the phrase. No comma should be used.

Two Adjectives Tests: Exercise A

Directions
In each sentence, insert commas where they should go. If the sentence is correct as written, write *correct* below it. Look at the lesson notes if you need help.

Again, be generous when correcting these exercises. Because "sounds right" is a subjective test, students may intentionally not have the same answers as those in the solutions—it may sound right to them. Discuss these answers with your student, and give them credit if they seem to have made a conscious choice about the answer they have given.

1) My friends and I went to the enormous, exciting playground near the library.

2) Sarah is my friend with long black hair.
    correct

3) Johnny has freckles and his hair is the color of a ripe, tasty carrot.

4) Naomi likes to wear denim overalls with bright, colorful patches on the knees.

5) I have the most wonderful, lively group of friends in the world!

Directions
Edit the errors in the following sentences using the editing marks that you have learned. Errors may be from this lesson or from the previous two lessons. There are five errors.

6) A good, old group of buddies is a wonderful thing. We like to hang out and, play with each other. We sometimes fight about, silly things. I suppose that happens in all groups of close, friends. We always make up and give each other a sincere, heartfelt apology.

3   EXERCISE A

Directions
In each sentence below, there is a comma split. All of the commas in each sentence and the lines below them are numbered. Identify the comma split and write its number in the space next to the sentence number. On the lines under each, write what the comma is splitting on the appropriate line. For the correctly placed commas, write the comma rule "buzzword" on the numbered line.

Example: _1_ We find, many fun, exciting things to do at the playground.
                        1   2

#1 _splits verb and direct object_

#2 _two adjectives tests_

_1_ 7) To get to the school, playground I go up the street, around the corner, and to the right.
                         1   2   3

#1 _splits noun and adjective_

#2 _items in a series_

#3 _items in a series_

_2_ 8) My wonderful, amazing dad, dropped me off there.
                    1   2

#1 _two adjectives tests_

#2 _splits subject and verb_

Commas—Two Adjectives Tests: Exercise B

Directions

In each sentence, insert commas where they should go. If the sentence is correct as written, write *correct* below it. Look at the lesson notes if you need help.

1) My friends and I had to decide which thrilling, enjoyable thing to do first!

2) Bouncy, joyful Sarah decided to start on the trampoline.

3) Calm, cool, collected Johnny chose the swings.

4) Daring, thrill-seeking Naomi wanted to try the super slide.

5) I wanted to do a loud, obnoxious gorilla impression on the monkey bars!

Directions

Edit the errors in the following sentences using the editing marks that you have learned. Errors may be from this lesson or from the previous two lessons. There are five errors.

6) We all decided it would be fun to see who could do the most outrageous, hilarious tricks. Sarah did flips, jumps, and kicks on the trampoline. I hung from the monkey bars by one leg. Naomi did a somersault off the end of the slide!

3 EXERCISE B

Directions
In each sentence below, there is a comma split. All of the commas in each sentence and the lines below them are numbered. Identify the comma split and write its number in the space next to the sentence number. On the lines under each, write what the comma is splitting on the appropriate line. For the correctly placed commas, write the comma rule "buzzword" on the numbered line.

_1_ 7) We were, mad at Naomi for her wild, dangerous stunt.
              1   2

  #1 _splits linking verb and complement_

  #2 _two adjectives tests_

_1_ 8) She, could have hurt her arm, leg, or head doing that trick!
            1   2   3

  #1 _splits subject and verb_

  #2 _items in a series_

  #3 _items in a series_

_2_ 9) Next time, reckless, foolish Naomi should do, a trick that is hilarious and safe.
                      1   2

  #1 _two adjectives tests_

  #2 _splits subject and verb_

Commas—Two Adjectives Tests: Exercise C

Directions
In each sentence, insert commas where they should go. If the sentence is correct as written, write *correct* below it. Look at the lesson notes if you need help.

1) All of a sudden, we felt a cool, blustery wind.

2) We could see the dark gray clouds coming toward us.
   correct

3) It had been such a bright, sunny morning!

4) Could there really be a wet, sloppy, soaking rainstorm coming?

5) We jumped like frightened, trembling mice when we heard the thunder give a tremendous, deafening crack!

Directions
Edit the errors in the following sentences using the editing marks that you have learned. Errors may be from this lesson or from the previous two lessons. There are five errors.

6) Not one of us/ had thought to bring an umbrella. We searched around the playground for a table, slide, or roof we could huddle under. There was one little old/ picnic table off to one side. We crouched under those splintered, stained/ pieces of wood to keep dry.

3   EXERCISE C

Directions

In each sentence below, there is a comma split. All of the commas in each sentence and the lines below them are numbered. Identify the comma split and write its number in the space next to the sentence number. On the lines under each, write what the comma is splitting on the appropriate line. For the correctly placed commas, write the comma rule "buzzword" on the numbered line.

__1__   7) Dad must have seen, the windy, wet rainstorm coming.
                                    1   2

    #1 _splits verb and direct object_

    #2 _two adjectives tests_

__1__   8) We, saw my dad's car come around the corner, up the driveway, and into the parking lot.
             1   2   3

    #1 _splits subject and verb_

    #2 _items in a series_

    #3 _items in a series_

__2__   9) Four soaked, shivering kids climbed into Dad's, car.
                        1   2

    #1 _two adjectives tests_

    #2 _splits noun and adjective_

Commas—Two Adjectives Tests: Assessment

Directions

In each sentence, insert commas where they should go. If the sentence is correct as written, write *correct* below it. Look at the lesson notes if you need help.

Each correctly placed comma is worth one point. If no correction is needed, it is worth one point.

___2___ 1) Dad's big, shiny, red car drove us to our house.

___1___ 2) The ragtag, dripping kids ran up to the front door.

___1___ 3) We were excited to see four cups of steaming hot chocolate!
                correct -1

___1___ 4) We wrapped towels around our shivering, wet shoulders.

___1___ 5) My friends and I gathered around the table in my warm, comfortable kitchen.

___4___
 6

Directions

Edit the errors in the following sentences using the editing marks that you have learned. Errors may be from this lesson or from the previous two lessons. There are five errors.

Each corrected error is worth one point.

6) Sarah got us all laughing, giggling, and snorting when she told us we looked like drowned rats. We had warmed up and were now telling funny, knee-slapping jokes to each other. Mom gave us each a chewy, gooey chocolate brownie to go with our hot chocolate.

___4___
 5

8/11

3 ASSESSMENT

Directions

In each sentence below, there is a comma split. All of the commas in each sentence and the lines below them are numbered. Identify the comma split and write its number in the space next to the sentence number. On the lines under each, write what the comma is splitting on the appropriate line. For the correctly placed commas, write the comma rule "buzzword" on the numbered line.

Identifying the comma split is worth two points. Identifying what is split and which comma buzzwords apply are worth one point each.

$\frac{2}{2}$ $\underline{\ 3\ }$ 7) Now our tummies were filled, our clothes were dry, and our bodies were, warmed.
                                              1   2   3

$\frac{0}{1}$ #1 *items in a series* _____

$\frac{1}{1}$ #2 *items in a series* _____

$\frac{0}{1}$ #3 *splits linking verb and complement* _____

$\frac{2}{2}$ $\underline{\ 1\ }$ 8) We, had a comical, strange, zany day!
                                     1   2   3

$\frac{1}{1}$ #1 *splits subject and verb* _____

$\frac{0}{1}$ #2 *two adjectives tests* _____

$\frac{0}{1}$ #3 *two adjectives tests* _____

$\frac{2}{2}$ $\underline{\ 1\ }$ 9) I am, lucky to have friends like Sarah, Johnny, and Naomi.
                                        1   2   3

$\frac{0}{1}$ #1 *splits linking verb and complement* _____

$\frac{1}{1}$ #2 *items in a series* _____

$\frac{1}{1}$ #3 *items in a series* _____

$\overline{\overline{15}}$

$\overline{\overline{26}}$ Total Points $\dfrac{21}{26} = 80\%$

Lesson 4
Commas—
Compound Sentences

Lesson 4: Commas—Compound Sentences

The buzzword for this rule is *compound sentence*.

Sometimes we will say or write two sentences, like this:

>I cleaned up my room. My sister washed the dishes.

This is fine; there's nothing wrong with the way these sentences are written. But sometimes it seems as though the sentences would read better if they were connected. If two sentences relate to each other, you can use a conjunction to do this:

>I cleaned up my room, and my sister washed the dishes.

The meaning is just a little different this way. By combining the sentences, you can show a relationship between them.

Compound sentence

A **compound sentence** is made of two or more sentences that are joined by a conjunction.

Use a comma before the conjunction when it joins two **independent clauses** (an **independent clause** is another name for a **sentence**). They're called independent clauses because they can stand alone, independently. They have, at minimum, a subject and a verb.

Be certain that you really have two independent clauses, though. You need to make sure that there is a subject and a verb in each one. If there isn't, you probably don't need a comma. Look at this example:

>I cleaned up my room and washed the dishes.

This is not a compound sentence; it is a sentence with a compound verb. In our example sentence here, there is only one subject, *I*, and *I* did both actions: **cleaned** and **washed**. There should not be a comma before the conjunction, because what comes after the conjunction, **washed the dishes**, is not a complete sentence.

One exception to the *compound sentence* rule:

>**IF** you are using the conjunction ***and***,
>
>>AND
>
>**IF** either of the sentences you are joining contains four words or fewer,

Do not use a comma.

>**Example:** I cleaned up my room and my sister vacuumed.

The second independent clause, ***my sister vacuumed***, only has three words. No comma is needed before ***and***.

Remember, this exception only applies when the conjunction is ***and***. If you used the same sentence as above, and substituted the conjunction ***but*** (or any other conjunction), you'd need a comma:

>I cleaned up my room, **but** my sister vacuumed.
>
>I could clean up my room, **or** my sister could vacuum.
>
>I didn't clean my room, **nor** did my sister vacuum.
>
>I didn't clean my room, **yet** my sister vacuumed.

Commas—Compound Sentences: Exercise A

Directions
In each sentence, insert commas where they should go. If the sentence is correct as written, write *correct* below it. Look at the lesson notes if you need help.

1) Our bodies are amazing things, and we should keep them healthy.

2) Every day I try to get some exercise, but sometimes my schedule gets too busy.

3) I enjoy playing basketball and biking with my friends.
   correct

4) There are many ways to exercise, and running is one of them.

5) A good game of tag is great exercise and it's fun!
   correct

Directions
Correct the following sentences using the editing marks that you have learned. Errors may be from this lesson or from earlier lessons. There are five errors.

6) I always make sure to carry cold ice water with me when I exercise. It's important to keep your body hydrated. I feel nauseated, dizzy, and ill when I get dehydrated. I don't like that feeling, and I do what I can to make sure that it doesn't happen. Hydrating is the best way to feel great while you play!

4   Exercise A

Directions

In each sentence below, there is a comma split. All of the commas in each sentence and the lines below them are numbered. Identify the comma split and write its number in the space next to the sentence number. On the lines under each, write what the comma is splitting on the appropriate line. For the correctly placed commas, write the comma rule "buzzword" on the numbered line.

_1_   7) I, enjoy aerobic, strengthening, and stretching exercises.
           1   2   3

     #1   _splits subject and verb_

     #2   _items in a series_

     #3   _items in a series_

_2_   8) I stretch for ten minutes, and I lift, weights for 20 minutes.
                          1   2

     #1   _compound sentence_

     #2   _splits verb and direct object_

_1_   9) A favorite, exercise of mine is fast, energetic dancing!
              1   2

     #1   _splits noun and adjective_

     #2   _two adjectives tests_

Commas—Compound Sentences: Exercise B

Directions

In each sentence, insert commas where they should go. If the sentence is correct as written, write *correct* below it. Look at the lesson notes if you need help.

1) My parents and I went to the lake this morning, and we went for a long walk.

2) I made sure to wear proper walking shoes and take my water bottle.
   correct

3) The trail around the lake was nice, and the fresh air felt great!

4) Mom walks fast, but I walk faster.

5) We took our dog and we all enjoyed the exercise.
   correct

Directions

Edit the following sentences using the editing marks that you have learned. Errors may be from this lesson or from earlier lessons. There are five errors.

6) Dogs∂ need exercise! Sparky loves to play fetch, chase his tail‸ and go for long walks. All of these things are great∂ exercise for him. Sparky is a healthy‸ happy dog. I love my dog∂ and my dog loves me.

4 EXERCISE B

Directions
In each sentence below, there is a comma split. All of the commas in each sentence and the lines below them are numbered. Identify the comma split and write its number in the space next to the sentence number. On the lines under each, write what the comma is splitting on the appropriate line. For the correctly placed commas, write the comma rule "buzzword" on the numbered line.

_1_ 7) We always, feed the ducks at the end of our long, lovely walk.
              1   2

   #1 _splits subject and verb_

   #2 _two adjectives tests_

_1_ 8) Mom takes, some tasty saltines, and I take the soft bread.
              1   2

   #1 _splits verb and direct object_

   #2 _compound sentence_

_3_ 9) The ducks quack, the seagulls dive, and the geese, squawk!
              1   2   3

   #1 _items in a series_

   #2 _items in a series_

   #3 _splits subject and verb_

Commas—Compound Sentences: Exercise C

Directions
In each sentence, insert commas where they should go. If the sentence is correct as written, write *correct* below it. Look at the lesson notes if you need help.

1) My dad's favorite exercise is playing basketball and I love playing soccer.
   correct

2) My sister likes hockey, but she doesn't get to play very often.

3) My brother is the quarterback for our football team, and he practices all the time.

4) Mom plays tennis and she competes in tournaments.
   correct

5) We all try to keep active and try to stay healthy.
   correct

Directions
Edit the following sentences using the editing marks that you have learned. Errors may be from this lesson or from earlier lessons. There are five errors.

6) It is always, important to be safe when you exercise. You'll need protection for your eyes, head, and body for some sports. Many people wear safety glasses. Football and ice hockey players wear pads, and helmets. Soccer players wear shin guards, and so do field hockey players.

4   EXERCISE C

Directions
In each sentence below, there is a comma split. All of the commas in each sentence and the lines below them are numbered. Identify the comma split and write its number in the space next to the sentence number. On the lines under each, write what the comma is splitting on the appropriate line. For the correctly placed commas, write the comma rule "buzzword" on the numbered line.

__1__ 7) Some, sports are played by teams, and some are played by individuals.
            1   2

   #1 _splits noun and adjective_

   #2 _compound sentence_

__1__ 8) Team sports and individual sports, are both great ways to break a strong, healthy sweat!
                                          1   2

   #1 _splits subject and verb_

   #2 _two adjectives tests_

__2__ 9) Playing sports is really entertaining, and the exercise is, good for you!
                                              1   2

   #1 _compound sentence_

   #2 _splits linking verb and complement_

Commas—Compound Sentences: Assessment

Directions

In each sentence, insert commas where they should go. If the sentence is correct as written, write *correct* below it. Look at the lesson notes if you need help.

Each correctly placed comma is worth one point. Identifying a sentence where a comma is not needed is worth one point.

   1)   There are a lot of ways to get exercise, but you have to make the effort.
   1

   2)   Don't take the elevator and walk where you can.
   1   *correct*

   3)   Ask your parents to park far away from your destination, and the walk will do you good!
   1

   4)   I've heard it said that each stair you climb adds time to your life, and I think it is true.
   1

   5)   Walking up stairs takes more time but gives you better health.
   1   *correct*

  2
  ―
  5

Directions

Edit the following sentences using the editing marks that you have learned. Errors may be from this lesson or from earlier lessons. There are five errors.

Each corrected error is worth one point.

6)   The worst part, about exercising is the stinky, sweaty clothes! Mom always yells at me if mine end up on the floor, the bed, or the countertop. I suppose that's what the hamper is for, and I, need to put them in there!

  4
  ―
  5

4 ASSESSMENT

Directions
In each sentence below, there is a comma split. All of the commas in each sentence and the lines below them are numbered. Identify the comma split and write its number in the space next to the sentence number. On the lines under each, write what the comma is splitting on the appropriate line. For the correctly placed commas, write the comma rule "buzzword" on the numbered line.

Identifying the comma split is worth two points. Identifying what is split and which comma buzzwords apply is worth one point each.

$\frac{0}{2}$ $\underline{\ 1\ }$ **7)** Put down the video game, controller, put on your shoes, and go outside and play tag.
　　　　　　　　　　　　　　　　　 1　　　　　　　 2　　　　　　　　3

　　　　$\frac{0}{1}$ #1 $\underline{\text{splits noun and adjective}\ }$

　　　　$\frac{0}{1}$ #2 $\underline{\text{items in a series}\ }$

　　　　$\frac{0}{1}$ #3 $\underline{\text{items in a series}\ }$

$\frac{2}{2}$ $\underline{\ 1\ }$ **8)** I, enjoy watching TV, but that's no way to get a strong, healthy body.
　　　　　　 1　　　　　　　 2　　　　　　　　　　　 3

　　　　$\frac{1}{1}$ #1 $\underline{\text{splits subject and verb}\ }$

　　　　$\frac{1}{1}$ #2 $\underline{\text{compound sentence}\ }$

　　　　$\frac{0}{1}$ #3 $\underline{\text{two adjectives tests}\ }$

$\frac{2}{2}$ $\underline{\ 1\ }$ **9)** I get, my heart rate up every day, and you should do the same thing!
　　　　　　　　 1　　　　　　　　　　　　 2

　　　　$\frac{0}{1}$ #1 $\underline{\text{splits verb and direct object}\ }$

　　　　$\frac{0}{1}$ #2 $\underline{\text{compound sentence}\ }$

$\overline{\overline{\ \ \ \ \ }}$
 14

$\overline{\overline{\ \ \ \ \ }}$ Total Points　$\dfrac{19}{24} = 80\%$
 24

Lesson 5
Commas—
Introductory Elements

Lesson 5: Commas—Introductory Elements

The buzzword for this rule is *introductory elements*.

An **introductory element** is a word or phrase that comes at the beginning of a sentence that makes it more interesting but that isn't essential to understanding the sentence. These elements are set apart from the rest of the sentence with a comma. Let's look at how these introductory elements work.

Introductory interjections

Interjections are words or sounds that express emotion: joy, sadness, confusion, anger, and so on. Interjections are often found at the beginning of a sentence. They don't have any grammatical job in a sentence—they are **nonessential**, or not necessary, to understanding the sentence. You could leave them off, and the sentence would still mean the same thing. Interjections are usually single words, but sometimes they are more than one word.

Examples: *Yes*, that's my favorite book!

Why, of course I'll come to dinner.

My goodness, that's not the right answer!

You can leave any of the interjections (*shown in italics*) off of the sentences above, and they would still mean the same things. Think about it like cooking: Interjections are an extra bit of seasoning that you can add to your sentences, but they are not the main course.

Introductory prepositional phrases

Put a comma after an introductory prepositional phrase. If there is more than one prepositional phrase at the beginning of a sentence, put the comma after the final one.

Examples: In the mail, packages arrived from my grandmother.

In the corner on the table, you'll find that letter.

Near the door in the stand with the umbrellas, you'll find your cane.

Commas—Introductory Elements: Exercise A

Directions

In each sentence, insert commas where they should go. If the sentence is correct as written, write *correct* below it. Look at the lesson notes if you need help.

1) In a corner of my room, there is my little bird's cage.

2) By the light of the morning sun, she chirps her good morning.

3) Oh, it's a great way to wake up to a new day!

4) Yes, my little songbird is a good friend.

5) In a little while, she'll sing again.

Directions

Edit the following sentences using the editing marks that you have learned. Errors may be from this lesson or from earlier lessons. There are five errors.

6) My little bird's name is Bella. She's a lovely, soft shade of yellow. On my last birthday in March, I asked for a pet. I knew a bird would be a great friend, and my mom and dad said I could have one. I told Mom and Dad that I would feed her, clean her cage, and groom her feathers.

5 EXERCISE A

Directions
In each sentence below, there is a comma split. All of the commas in each sentence and the lines below them are numbered. Identify the comma split and write its number in the space next to the sentence number. On the lines under each, write what the comma is splitting on the appropriate line. For the correctly placed commas, write the comma rule "buzzword" on the numbered line.

__1__ 7) My, family has always had a cat, a dog, or a bird.
         1   2   3

  #1 *splits noun and adjective*

  #2 *items in a series*

  #3 *items in a series*

__2__ 8) On the couch in our living room, you, will find our fluffy, lazy cat.
                                        1   2   3

  #1 *introductory element*

  #2 *splits subject and verb*

  #3 *two adjectives tests*

__3__ 9) Yes, Heathcliff sheds a lot, but we love, him.
          1   2   3

  #1 *introductory element*

  #2 *compound sentence*

  #3 *splits verb and direct object*

Commas—Introductory Elements: Exercise B

Directions
In each sentence, insert commas where they should go. If the sentence is correct as written, write *correct* below it. Look at the lesson notes if you need help.

1) Why, I would have never thought of having a snake as a pet!

2) On a table in my friend's room, you'll see her snake.

3) Yes, his name really is Snuggles.

4) In the wild, snakes might attack.

5) No, Snuggles would never do that!

Directions
Edit the following sentences using the editing marks that you have learned. Errors may be from this lesson or from earlier lessons. There are five errors.

6) Some people have ferrets, pigs, or lizards as pets. An animal may seem like a strange pet to you, but another person may love that animal as a pet. Giving a pet a loving, caring home is very important. In the end, that is all that matters.

5 EXERCISE B

Directions
In each sentence below, there is a comma split. All of the commas in each sentence and the lines below them are numbered. Identify the comma split and write its number in the space next to the sentence number. On the lines under each, write what the comma is splitting on the appropriate line. For the correctly placed commas, write the comma rule "buzzword" on the numbered line.

_1_ 7) Snuggles got out of his, cage one afternoon, and he went on a mission to explore my
                                1   2
   friend's huge, two-story house.
                3

   #1 _splits noun and adjective_

   #2 _compound sentence_

   #3 _two adjectives tests_

_2_ 8) Well, we found, him curled up in her dad's comfy chair!
             1   2

   #1 _introductory element_

   #2 _splits verb and direct object_

_1_ 9) At least he, wasn't eating chips, watching a movie, and drinking a root beer!
                   1   2   3

   #1 _splits subject and verb_

   #2 _items in a series_

   #3 _items in a series_

Commas—Introductory Elements: Exercise C

Directions
In each sentence, insert commas where they should go. If the sentence is correct as written, write *correct* below it. Look at the lesson notes if you need help.

1) For my birthday in January, my parents got me a dog!

2) Yes, I had been dreaming about and hoping for a dog for years.

3) During my search for the perfect dog, I discovered greyhounds.

4) After rescue from racing, greyhounds need loving homes.

5) Oh, I was so excited to finally have a greyhound of my own!

Directions
Edit the following sentences using the editing marks that you have learned. Errors may be from this lesson or from earlier lessons. There are five errors.

6) Greyhounds have long, sleek bodies, and they are designed to run fast. Yes, these dogs are speedy, but they are gentle. Greyhounds are bred to race and are usually adopted as adult dogs when they retire. These dogs are so happy to be loved, cared for, and protected within a family.

5 EXERCISE C

Directions
In each sentence below, there is a comma split. All of the commas in each sentence and the lines below them are numbered. Identify the comma split and write its number in the space next to the sentence number. On the lines under each, write what the comma is splitting on the appropriate line. For the correctly placed commas, write the comma rule "buzzword" on the numbered line.

__2__ 7) In the morning after breakfast, my friend and I will take our dogs to the dog, park.
                                         1   2

#1 _introductory element_

#2 _splits noun and adjective_

__2__ 8) It's great to see the dogs exercise and play, and we, love spending time with them.
                                                        1   2

#1 _compound sentence_

#2 _splits subject and verb_

__1__ 9) Our, dogs run, play fetch, and chase each other all morning at the dog park!
           1   2   3

#1 _splits noun and adjective_

#2 _items in a series_

#3 _items in a series_

Commas—Introductory Elements: Assessment

Directions

In each sentence, insert commas where they should go. If the sentence is correct as written, write *correct* below it. Look at the lesson notes if you need help.

Each correctly placed comma is worth one point.

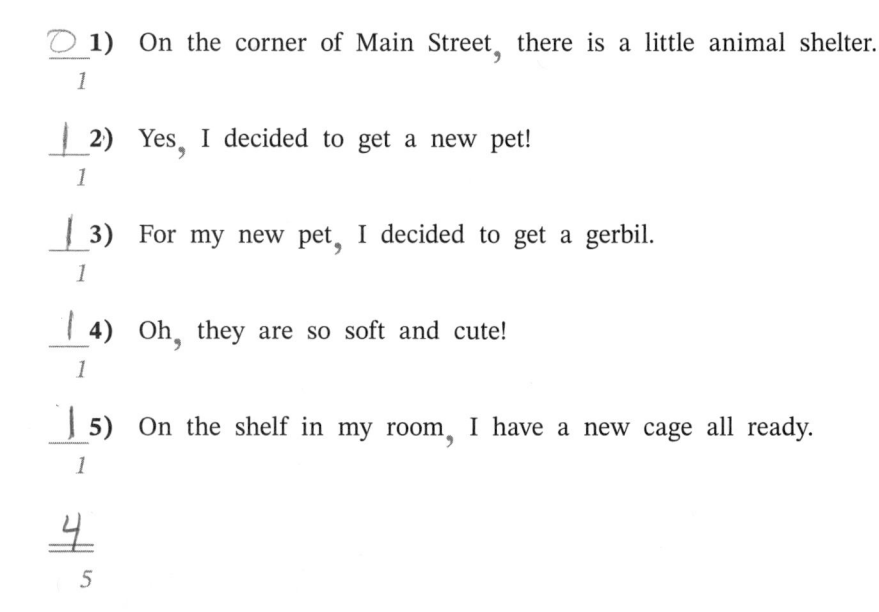

1) On the corner of Main Street, there is a little animal shelter.

2) Yes, I decided to get a new pet!

3) For my new pet, I decided to get a gerbil.

4) Oh, they are so soft and cute!

5) On the shelf in my room, I have a new cage all ready.

Directions

Edit the following sentences using the editing marks that you have learned. Errors may be from this lesson or from earlier lessons. There are five errors.

Each corrected error is worth one point.

6) My trip to the animal shelter was a lot of fun, but it made me feel sad, too. In the cages, there were dogs, cats, and even mice. Oh, I wanted to take them all home with me! I wish all animals could find good homes, and I'm going to make sure my pets are well taken care of.

5 ASSESSMENT

Directions

In each sentence below, there is a comma split. All of the commas in each sentence and the lines below them are numbered. Identify the comma split and write its number in the space next to the sentence number. On the lines under each, write what the comma is splitting on the appropriate line. For the correctly placed commas, write the comma rule "buzzword" on the numbered line.

Identifying the comma split is worth two points. Identifying what is split and which comma buzzwords apply is worth one point each.

$\frac{2}{2}$ $\underline{2}$ 7) Well, my animal shelter trip was, an interesting, moving experience.
                                      1   2   3

      $\frac{O}{1}$ #1 *introductory element* _____

      $\frac{1}{1}$ #2 *splits linking verb and complement* _____

      $\frac{O}{1}$ #3 *two adjectives tests* _____

$\frac{2}{2}$ $\underline{1}$ 8) All of the animals, had sweet faces, cuddly bodies, and huge eyes.
                             1   2   3

      $\frac{O}{1}$ #1 *splits subject and verb* _____

      $\frac{O}{1}$ #2 *items in a series* _____

      $\frac{O}{1}$ #3 *items in a series* _____

$\frac{2}{2}$ $\underline{3}$ 9) From the bottom of my heart, I wanted to adopt them all, but my mom said, no.
                                                     1   2   3

      $\frac{O}{1}$ #1 *introductory element* _____

      $\frac{O}{1}$ #2 *compound sentence* _____

      $\frac{O}{1}$ #3 *splits verb and direct object* _____

$\frac{6}{15}$

$\frac{14}{25}$ Total Points $\frac{20}{25} = 80\%$

Lesson 6
Commas—Interrupters

Lesson 6: Commas—Interrupters

In this lesson, we will be learning two buzzwords for the comma rules about **interrupters**. **Interrupters** are just what they sound like—they are words or phrases that *interrupt* a sentence.

In the last lesson, you learned about **introductory elements** that can be left out of a sentence without changing the meaning. The same is true of **interrupters**. They are **nonessential** to the meaning of a sentence—they can be left out, and the sentence still means the same thing. The difference is that **interrupters** can come anywhere in a sentence, not just at the beginning.

Interrupters are *set off* from the rest of the sentence. That means that there will be commas before, after, or on both sides of the interrupter, depending on where it is located in the sentence. Let's look at two different kinds of interrupters and examples of each:

1) The buzzword for this rule is **direct address**.

    Direct address is when you are speaking to someone and you use their name in the sentence. Look at the examples below to see how direct address is set off by commas, depending on where it comes in the sentence:

    James, where do you think you're going? (*The comma goes* **after** *the direct address at the beginning.*)

    Where, James, do you think you're going? (*Commas go* **before and after** *the direct address in the middle of the sentence.*)

    Where do you think you're going, James? (*The comma goes* **before** *the direct address at the end.*)

    You could substitute a nickname (sweetie, kiddo, pookie pie, etc.) or another form of address (old buddy, my dear Ms. Smith, my fellow students, etc.) but you should still set the direct address apart with commas.

2) The buzzword for this rule is **expression**.

    The English language uses a lot of expressions, such as *for example, by the way, on the other hand, therefore,* and *in other words*. We use them to give the reader or listener clues to know where our communication is going.

    Example: There are reasons I won't let you go swimming right now. For example, you just ate a big meal.

    (The comma goes **after** the expression *for example*.)

    You could remove *for example* from the second sentence and it would still mean the same thing. But the sentence is clearer about its purpose with this expression included: the speaker has more reasons why they will not let the listener go swimming, but this is one example.

    You could also write the second sentence like this:

    You, for example, just ate a big meal. (Commas go **before and after** the expression *for example*.)

    Or like this:

    You just ate a big meal, for example. (The comma goes **before** the expression *for example*.)

> **Note:** An expression at the beginning of a sentence can sometimes be considered an **introductory element**, like we learned about in the last lesson. That's okay; just make sure to put a comma after it, and you will be correct no matter which it is!

Even though interrupters are not essential to understanding a sentence, that doesn't mean that they don't make sentences better! They can explain more about a sentence or add emotion or interest. The next time you are writing something, think about whether an interrupter can make your writing more interesting!

6 EXERCISE A

Commas—Interrupters: Exercise A

Directions
In each sentence, insert commas where they should go. Look at the lesson notes if you need help.

1) Lucas, have you written the thank-you notes for your birthday gifts?

2) You did, after all, get a fantastic new video game from Nana.

3) I can't find a good pen, Mom.

4) By the way, can you find me Nana's address?

5) I put all of the stuff you need on the desk in your room last night, dear.

Directions
Edit the following sentences using the editing marks that you have learned. Errors may be from this lesson or from earlier lessons. There are five errors.

6) I got all of my thank-you notes written last night. I sat right down at my desk, got out my paper and pen, and got to work. Yes, it seems like a lot of work, but it really is important to thank people when they get you a gift. I really feel good when I get my thank-you notes written and mailed.

Exercise A 6

Directions

In each sentence below, there is a comma split. All of the commas in each sentence and the lines below them are numbered. Identify the comma split and write its number in the space next to the sentence number. On the lines under each, write what the comma is splitting on the appropriate line. For the correctly placed commas, write the comma rule "buzzword" on the numbered line.

__1__ 7) For my eighth, birthday I got a bike, a skateboard, and a couple of great video games.
             1   2   3

   #1 _splits noun and adjective_

   #2 _items in a series_

   #3 _items in a series_

__1__ 8) My favorite, is my shiny new bike that, by the way, I've been wanting forever!
              1   2   3

   #1 _splits subject and verb_

   #2 _expression_

   #3 _expression_

__2__ 9) At the end of our road, we have an empty lot where the guys in the neighborhood have
                                1

built, a bike track.
     2

   #1 _introductory element_

   #2 _splits verb and direct object_

6 EXERCISE B

Commas—Interrupters: Exercise B

Directions
In each sentence, insert commas where they should go. Look at the lesson notes if you need help.

1) Oh boy, my little sister is having her birthday next week!

2) Sarah, what theme did you choose for your party?

3) A pirate theme, I'm sure, is something all of your friends will like.

4) Pink and purple are great colors, little sis.

5) If I chose the colors, on the other hand, I'd pick orange and blue.

Directions
Edit the following sentences using the editing marks that you have learned. Errors may be from this lesson or from earlier lessons. There are five errors.

6) I can't wait to go to my sister's party, and help her celebrate. There will be cake, balloons, and party games. I am most excited about the cake! I don't mind playing the little kid games, but I hope I don't have to wear a funny pirate hat.

EXERCISE B **6**

Directions

In each sentence below, there is a comma split. All of the commas in each sentence and the lines below them are numbered. Identify the comma split and write its number in the space next to the sentence number. On the lines under each, write what the comma is splitting on the appropriate line. For the correctly placed commas, write the comma rule "buzzword" on the numbered line.

_1_ 7) I saved, my money to buy Sarah a beautiful, delicate doll.
            1   2

   #1 _splits verb and direct object_

   #2 _two adjectives tests_

_2_ 8) Oh, I, was so excited to give it to her, and I made sure to wrap the present with care.
       1 2   3

   #1 _introductory element_

   #2 _splits subject and verb_

   #3 _compound sentence_

_3_ 9) She opened the gift, my friend, and her, eyes lit up!
                              1   2   3

   #1 _direct address_

   #2 _direct address_

   #3 _splits noun and adjective_

6 EXERCISE C

Commas—Interrupters: Exercise C

Directions
In each sentence, insert commas where they should go. Look at the lesson notes if you need help.

1) Now, my little sister, is the time to write your thank-you notes.

2) Just to be clear, wouldn't you like to be thanked for the gifts you give?

3) Get some cards with pirates on them, little friend.

4) How many cards do you need to write, for crying out loud?

5) If you have that many cards, buddy, I'll help, and we'll finish them over the next few days.

Directions
Edit the following sentences using the editing marks that you have learned. Errors may be from this lesson or from earlier lessons. There are five errors.

6) Any task is easier if you divide it up into easy, doable steps. You may have forty notes to write, but breaking that into five notes a day makes it easier to do. It is important to say "thank you" to people who gave you a gift. I always make a list, write a note, and check off each name. The job is more fun that way!

Exercise C 6

Directions

In each sentence below, there is a comma split. All of the commas in each sentence and the lines below them are numbered. Identify the comma split and write its number in the space next to the sentence number. On the lines under each, write what the comma is splitting on the appropriate line. For the correctly placed commas, write the comma rule "buzzword" on the numbered line.

_1_ 7) I helped, my sister make a fun, colorful chart to track her thank-you notes.
                    1   2

   #1 _splits verb and direct object_

   #2 _two adjectives tests_

_1_ 8) She, wrote five thank you-notes, and I rewarded her with a star on the chart.
                1   2

   #1 _splits subject and verb_

   #2 _compound sentence_

_2_ 9) Well, those notes, were written in no time at all!
             1   2

   #1 _introductory element_

   #2 _splits subject and verb_

6 ASSESSMENT

Commas—Interrupters: Assessment

Directions

In each sentence, insert commas where they should go. Look at the lesson notes if you need help.

Each correctly placed comma is worth one point.

$\frac{1}{1}$ 1) My friends, it is easy to put off writing thank-you notes.

$\frac{O}{1}$ 2) Of course, you could always make a quick phone call instead.

$\frac{2}{2}$ 3) You, my computer-literate pal, can even send an email.

$\frac{1}{2}$ 4) Phone calls and emails, however, don't give the same feeling as a note.

$\frac{1}{2}$ 5) Do you remember, by any chance, how you felt the last time you got a personal letter?

$\frac{5}{8}$

Directions

Edit the following sentences using the editing marks that you have learned. Errors may be from this lesson or from earlier lessons. There are five errors.

Each corrected error is worth one point.

6) The mail comes to my house in the late/ afternoon. I always run out, open the mailbox⌄, and grab the mail. Right on top was a bright ⨯yellow⨯ envelope⌃, and it was addressed to me! On the back of the envelope⌃, I saw my little niece's return address. I got a huge smile on my face when I/ saw her thank-you note!

$\frac{2}{5}$

ASSESSMENT 6

Directions

In each sentence below, there is a comma split. All of the commas in each sentence and the lines below them are numbered. Identify the comma split and write its number in the space next to the sentence number. On the lines under each, write what the comma is splitting on the appropriate line. For the correctly placed commas, write the comma rule "buzzword" on the numbered line.

Identifying the comma split is worth two points. Identifying what is split and which comma buzzwords apply is worth one point each.

2 / 2   **2**   7) Hey, what did you get for your, birthday, Madeleine?
                    1   2   3

    1/1 #1 _introductory element_

    0/1 #2 _splits noun and adjective_

    0/1 #3 _direct address_

2 / 2   **1**   8) She, sent me a soft, warm winter jacket, but it's too big right now.
                    1   2   3

    1/1 #1 _splits subject and verb_

    1/1 #2 _two adjectives tests_

    0/1 #3 _compound sentence_

2 / 2   **4**   9) By the beginning of winter, I'll grow into it, of course, and it'll be, great!
                                                1   2   3   4

    0/1 #1 _introductory element_

    0/1 #2 _expression_

    0/1 #3 _expression_

    1/1 #4 _splits linking verb and complement_

10 / 16

17 / 29 Total Points $\dfrac{23}{29} = 80\%$

Lesson 7
Commas—Names, Dates, & Places

Lesson 7: Commas—Names, Dates, & Places

These are the last two comma rules to learn in this program! There are times when we're writing when we want to talk about places, dates, and people's names. There are special rules for commas in some of these situations.

The buzzword for these rules is **names, dates, & places**.

Names and abbreviations

Do you know anyone who is named after someone else in their family? Some families have the tradition of passing down names from one generation to the next. Many times, this results in people having something like *Jr., Sr.,* or *III* after their names. Other times, people have additions to their names because they have earned a special degree at a university or college. In this case, you could see letters like *MD* (medical doctor), *Esq.* (short for *Esquire* and used by some lawyers), or *PhD* (doctor of philosophy) after that person's name.

Place a comma between the name and the letters following it if the letters are for something a person has earned. Don't put a comma before letters or numerals that are part of a person's given name. Here are some examples:

| Robert Downey Jr. | James Yoffe, MD | Juliana Smith, Esq. |
| Henry V | William Clemons IV | Alice Chen, PhD |

Dates and addresses

When we write out specific dates and addresses in sentences, there are some helpful comma rules that we use. The commas are there to separate the different parts of the date or address. **Don't** use a comma:

- between the month and the day.
- between the street number and the name of the street.
- between the state and the zip code.

Examples: On January 20, 2020, we moved to 123 Main Street, Raleigh, North Carolina 27613.

My family moved to Raleigh, North Carolina, on Tuesday, January 20, 2020.

> **Note:** When a date or address is in the middle of a sentence, put a comma after the last part of it. Look at the commas in the sentences above, after *2020* in the first one and after *North Carolina* in the second.

Commas—Names, Dates, & Places: Exercise A

Directions
Put commas where they should go in each of the following sentences. Look at the lesson notes if you need help.

1) I was born in Los Angeles, California, on January 20, 1993.

2) In 2001, my family and I moved to 2830 Chesapeake Avenue, Anchorage, Alaska 99516.

3) My family lived in Anchorage, Alaska, for many years.

4) After I graduated from high school on May 23, 2011, I left for college in Pullman, Washington.

5) The next year, I switched schools and moved to Las Vegas, Nevada, to complete my college degree.

Directions
Edit the following sentences using the editing marks that you have learned. Errors may be from this lesson or from earlier lessons. There are five errors.

6) Living in Las Vegas, Nevada, was a lot of fun! I was a singing waitress there. On May 19, 2016, I walked across the stage to receive the degree that I had earned. That was a great feeling! I will remember with fondness my exciting, fun-filled time in college.

7 EXERCISE A

Directions
In each sentence below, there is a comma split. All of the commas in each sentence and the lines below them are numbered. Identify the comma split and write its number in the space next to the sentence number. On the lines under each, write what the comma is splitting on the appropriate line. For the correctly placed commas, write the comma rule "buzzword" on the numbered line.

__1__ 7) I, went home to Anchorage, Alaska, in the summer of 2016.
           1   2   3

    #1 _splits subject and verb_

    #2 _names, dates, & places_

    #3 _names, dates, & places_

__1__ 8) My address again became, 2830 Chesapeake Avenue, Anchorage, Alaska 99516.
                                   1   2   3

    #1 _splits linking verb and complement_

    #2 _names, dates, & places_

    #3 _names, dates, & places_

__2__ 9) By the middle of 2017, I was ready to follow in the footsteps of my, uncles and join the
                             1   2

Air Force.

    #1 _introductory element_

    #2 _splits noun and adjective_

Commas—Names, Dates, & Places: Exercise B

Directions

Put commas where they should go in each of the following sentences. If the sentence is correct, write *correct* below it. Look at the lesson notes if you need help.

1) My oldest uncle's name is Donald Gene Travers III.

    correct

2) His father was Donald Gene Travers Jr.

    correct

3) My uncle became a lawyer, and then he wrote his name as Donald Gene Travers, Esq.

4) This trend continued when I married my husband, Robert Carlos Jimenez Jr.

5) We named our son Robert Carlos Jimenez III.

    correct

Directions

Edit the following sentences using the editing marks that you have learned. Errors may be from this lesson or from earlier lessons. There are five errors.

6) Both of my uncles served in the Air Force. After college, I was inspired to serve my country, and I began to look around for a way to do that. I went to the library, looked up all sorts of books on women in the military, and read for days on the subject. I shocked my parents when I told them I had decided on the Air Force. To tell the truth, they thought that I was too stubborn to be interested in such a career!

7 EXERCISE B

Directions
In each sentence below, there is a comma split. All of the commas in each sentence and the lines below them are numbered. Identify the comma split and write its number in the space next to the sentence number. On the lines under each, write what the comma is splitting on the appropriate line. For the correctly placed commas, write the comma rule "buzzword" on the numbered line.

__1__ 7) My decision to join the Air Force, one was one of the best, most important decisions of my life.
                                              1   2

   #1 _splits subject and verb_

   #2 _two adjectives tests_

__3__ 8) I learned discipline, acquired leadership skills, and developed a deep, love of my country.
                              1   2   3

   #1 _items in a series_

   #2 _items in a series_

   #3 _splits noun and adjective_

__1__ 9) My first duty station was, Cape Canaveral, Florida, where they launch the space shuttles.
                                   1   2   3

   #1 _splits linking verb and complement_

   #2 _names, dates, & places_

   #3 _names, dates, & places_

Commas—Names, Dates, & Places: Exercise C

Directions
Put commas where they should go in each of the following sentences. If the sentence is correct, write *correct* below it. Look at the lesson notes if you need help.

1) My husband's father's name is Robert Carlos Jimenez Sr.
   correct

2) On June 30, 2020, he retired from his engineering career and moved to 333 Palm Avenue, Miami, Florida.

3) He and his wife love to play with Robert Carlos Jimenez III.
   correct

4) We call him Robbie and he livens up our days at 1234 Long Lane, Lititz, Pennsylvania.

5) Maybe someday little Robbie will grow up to be Robert Carlos Jimenez, MD!

Directions
Edit the following sentences using the editing marks that you have learned. Errors may be from this lesson or from earlier lessons. There are five errors.

6) Robbie's favorite things in the world right now are trains. As a matter of fact, he even has trains on his pajamas! On the floor in the living room, he loves to set up his train tracks and play with all of his trains. We get him to eat his vegetables by pretending that they are train cars. "Robbie, here comes a green train engine! Choo-choo!"

7 EXERCISE C

Directions
In each sentence below, there is a comma split. All of the commas in each sentence and the lines below them are numbered. Identify the comma split and write its number in the space next to the sentence number. On the lines under each, write what the comma is splitting on the appropriate line. For the correctly placed commas, write the comma rule "buzzword" on the numbered line.

__3__ 7) Class, today we are going to learn about ancient, time-honored, traditions involving names.
            1   2   3

#1 _direct address_

#2 _two adjectives tests_

#3 _splits noun and adjective_

__2__ 8) For many years, we have given sons, the names of their fathers, but there are certain rules.
            1   2   3

#1 _introductory element_

#2 _splits indirect object and direct object_

#3 _compound sentence_

__2__ 9) Yes, a comma, goes between a name and an earned title but not between a name and
        1   2

a Roman numeral.

#1 _introductory element_

#2 _splits subject and verb_

Commas—Names, Dates, & Places: Assessment

Directions
Put commas where they should go in each of the following sentences. If the sentence is correct, write *correct* below it. Look at the lesson notes if you need help.

Each correctly placed comma is worth one point. Identifying a sentence where a comma is not needed is worth one point.

0/1 1) The last queen of England was Queen Elizabeth II.
     correct

0/1 2) My nephew's name is George Evans Jr., and he's an expert on British royalty.

0/2 3) Queen Elizabeth's main address was Buckingham Palace, London, England.

1/2 4) On June 3, 2019, he saw the Queen's house up close when he went to London.

3/4 5) He stayed in England until June 17, 2019, and then he returned home to 150 Elm Circle, Birmingham, Alabama.

4/10

Directions
Edit the following sentences using the editing marks that you have learned. Errors may be from this lesson or from earlier lessons. There are five errors.

Each corrected error is worth one point.

6) Henry VIII was an interesting English king but he wasn't a very nice man. The most famous thing about him is his six wives. His wives were Catherine of Aragon, Anne Boleyn, Jane Seymour, Anne of Cleves, Katherine Howard and Catherine Parr. His first three wives went through tremendous painful struggles to give the king a son. There was a great celebration when his son Edward was born.

2/5

7 ASSESSMENT

Directions

In each sentence below, there is a comma split. All of the commas in each sentence and the lines below them are numbered. Identify the comma split and write its number in the space next to the sentence number. On the lines under each, write what the comma is splitting on the appropriate line. For the correctly placed commas, write the comma rule "buzzword" on the numbered line.

Identifying the comma split is worth two points. Identifying what is split and which comma buzzwords apply is worth one point each.

$\frac{2}{2}$ _2_ 7) Students, today we, will talk about Anne Boleyn, and she was Henry VIII's second wife.
　　　　　　　　　　　　1　　　　　2　　　　　　　　　　　　　　3

　　　$\frac{0}{1}$ #1 *direct address* _____

　　　$\frac{2}{1}$ #2 *splits subject and verb* _____

　　　$\frac{0}{1}$ #3 *compound sentence* _____

$\frac{0}{2}$ _2_ 8) To say the least, her desire was to fulfill the king's most heartfelt, wish for a son.
　　　　　　　　　　　　　1　　　　　　　　　　　　　　　　　　　　　　2

　　　$\frac{0}{1}$ #1 *introductory element* _____

　　　$\frac{0}{1}$ #2 *splits adjective and noun* _____

$\frac{2}{2}$ _2_ 9) No, she did not have, a Henry Jr., but she did give birth to England's greatest queen
　　　　　　　　　　　1　　　　　　　2　　　3

　　　named Elizabeth I.

　　　$\frac{0}{1}$ #1 *introductory element* _____

　　　$\frac{1}{1}$ #2 *splits verb and direct object* _____

　　　$\frac{1}{1}$ #3 *compound sentence* _____

$\frac{=}{14}$

$\overline{\overline{}}$ Total Points　$\dfrac{23}{29} = 80\%$
29

Lesson 8
Direct Quotations

Lesson 8: Direct Quotations

When you're reading something, there are punctuation marks that let you know who is speaking and what they're saying.

"Bill, I want to go home," said John.

In the sentence above, who is speaking? That's right: **John**. The sentence inside the quotation marks, *Bill, I want to go home*, is what he said. We use quotation marks to show exactly what someone said.

Here's the next sentence in the little story:

"John, I was hoping to stay a little longer," I replied.

In this sentence, *I* am speaking. Since John was speaking to Bill and *I* replied, we know that *I* must be Bill.

These are quotation marks: " " They always come in pairs, and they always go around the words that people speak. The first set of quotation marks is sometimes referred to as the **open quote mark**, and the second one, at the end of the direct quote, is the **close quote mark**. Whatever is inside the quotation marks (words and punctuation) is called **dialogue** or simply the **quote**. The part of the sentence that shows us who is speaking, like *said John* or *I replied*, is called the **narrative**. The narrative tells us who is speaking and sometimes gives us more information about what is happening. Here's an example of narrative that provides more information:

As I walked into the house, I yelled, "Is anybody here?"

There are a few guidelines for using quotation marks. Read through the following examples and look back at them as you complete the exercises if you need help.

A) Always begin the dialogue with a capital letter if the quote is a complete sentence:

James said, "**T**ell me more about your trip."

Tell me more about your trip is a complete sentence, so it must begin with a capital letter.

B) Sometimes the narrative is placed in the middle of the dialogue, like this:

"I was really hoping," said Pam, "that you would come."

The complete sentence that is quoted is *I was really hoping that you would come.* Notice that *that* isn't capitalized even though it's the first word in the second part of the quote. That's because it's in the middle of the sentence being quoted.

But what about this example?:

"I am glad that I could make it," I said to Pam. "I was able to change my other commitment."

I am glad that I could make it is a complete sentence. That's why there is a period after *Pam*. Then the next sentence of dialogue, *I was able to change my other commitment*, begins with a capital letter and ends with a period.

C) Sometimes the speaker has more than one sentence to say all at once, like this:

Janie exclaimed, "The state fair is great! Don't you want to go? I sure do!"

Janie said several sentences, and they are all enclosed together by one pair of quotation marks. You only need one pair, even if the dialogue is fourteen sentences long!

Let's talk a little bit about the other punctuation marks in sentences with direct quotations. Notice that, in addition to quotation marks, the narrative and dialogue are set apart from each other with one or two commas. Commas and quotation marks are almost always used together. Here are the guidelines for commas, periods, and other end-of-sentence punctuation:

- If the narrative is at the **beginning** of or the **end** of the sentence, it is set apart by **one comma**.

    Examples: Bob said, "I wish I could go to the state fair."

    "I wish I could go to the state fair," said Bob.

- Do you notice anything about the period at the end of the quote in the sentences above? Bob is making a statement, and it's a complete sentence, so the quote needs a period, right? Yes, and it has one in the first sentence. But what about the second one? There is a comma at the end of the quote, not a period! That's because two periods, one at the end of the quote and one at the end of the sentence, would be confusing. Look:

    "I wish I could go to the state fair." said Bob.

    A period is a signal to the reader to come to a full stop, so the reader comes to a full stop after *fair*. But then the sentence continues—there's no capital letter, and there's another full stop after *Bob*. So, here's how that problem is solved: we change the period at the end of the quote to a comma! That way, the reader understands that the sentence continues after the quote.

    "I wish I could go to the state fair," said Bob.

- If the narrative comes in the middle of the quoted sentence, put a comma both before and after the narrative:

    "It would be so much fun," sighed Bob, "to eat the good food and ride some rides."

    Because *sighed Bob* is interrupting the sentence, it is punctuated like any other interrupter in the middle of a sentence: with a comma before it and another after.

- The punctuation at the end of a quote is only changed to a comma if it is a statement that would end with a period. If it is a question or an exclamation, leave the question mark or exclamation point so the reader knows what kind of sentence it is:

    "Why can't you go?" Janie asked Bob.

    "I have three basketball games that week!" cried Bob.

The buzzword for commas used in sentences with direct quotes is *gear-change comma*. That's because it is a signal to the reader that the content of the sentence is changing, either from dialogue to narrative or from narrative to dialogue.

> In American English, punctuation at the end of a quote goes **inside** the quotation marks. Whether the quote ends in a comma, a period, a question mark, or an exclamation point, put them inside the second set of quotation marks.

When you are editing, here are the signs you will use to show that quotation marks are needed or that a word should be capitalized:

I said, ˬ"this is my quote.ˬ"

These are the signs for "add quotes": ˬ" and ˬ"

This is the sign to capitalize a letter: ☰

8 EXERCISE A

Direct Quotations: Exercise A

Directions
The sentences below include all of the punctuation marks they need, *except* for the quotation marks. Read each sentence and add the quotation marks where they belong. Look back at the lesson notes if you need help.

1) Juan looked at his best friend Jason and asked, "Do you ever think about being a grownup?"

2) "Yeah," Jason said. "It's kind of scary, isn't it?"

3) "There's a lot to learn," said Juan. "You have to learn about money, for example. Do you ever save money?"

4) "My mom and dad pay me for doing chores," said Jason, "and I save one-third of it for college and one-third of it for gifts. I get to spend the rest on whatever I want."

5) "That's pretty cool!" Juan exclaimed. "I think I'll talk to my parents about that."

Directions
Edit the following sentences, using the editing marks you have learned. There are five errors. (Because quotation marks always come in pairs, missing quotation marks count as one error, but make sure you put in both sets.)

6) Maddie is too young to learn about saving money, but a year from now she will begin to learn about saving. She's still learning the differences among pennies, nickels, dimes, and quarters. Once, I gave her three pennies and I had one quarter. She said, "I have more monies than you do!"

Directions

In each sentence below, there is a comma split. All of the commas in each sentence and the lines below them are numbered. Identify the comma split and write its number in the space next to the sentence number. On the lines under each, write what the comma is splitting on the appropriate line. For the correctly placed commas, write the comma rule "buzzword" on the numbered line. For quotation marks, write *quotation marks*. Since each pair of quotation marks only counts as one thing, there will only be a number under the first quotation mark.

___1___ 7) Maddie's first, chores will be putting her toys away, making her bed, and setting the table.
               1   2   3

#1 _splits noun and adjective_

#2 _items in a series_

#3 _items in a series_

___2___ 8) Yes, Maddie must do, all her chores, and she'll be paid one dollar a day.
           1   2   3

#1 _introductory element_

#2 _splits verb and direct object_

#3 _compound sentence_

___2___ 9) At the end of the day, she, must put away her toys after Mom says only once, "Maddie,
                                 1   2   3 4

put your toys away."

#1 _introductory element_

#2 _splits subject and verb_

#3 _gear-change comma_

#4 _quotation marks_

8 EXERCISE B

Direction Quotations: Exercise B

Directions

In this activity, you must put in all of the punctuation that is needed, including the quotation marks and some commas (we've provided some for you). Read each of the following sentences carefully and insert punctuation where it should go. (**Hint:** Don't forget to check the end of the sentence!) Look back at the lesson notes if you need help.

1) Juan said, "Hey, Jason, I talked to my parents about being paid for my chores."

2) "Well, what did they say?" asked Jason.

3) "They said we'll start the whole program on Friday," said Juan.

4) "What chores do you have to do?" Jason asked.

5) "I have to make my bed, put my dirty clothes in the hamper, put away my clean clothes, and clear the table after dinner," said Juan. "Now, let's ride our bikes!"

Directions

Edit the following sentences, using the editing marks you have learned. There are five errors. (Because quotation marks always come in pairs, missing quotation marks count as one error, but make sure you put in both sets.)

6) Juan, needless to say, knows the value of different coins and bills. He is older than Maddie. He has four chores to do each day, and he must do them without having to be told more than once. He began his savings program on Friday, January 7, 2022. His parents will give him three dollars for spending and six dollars to be divided between his college and gift savings account.

EXERCISE B **8**

Directions
In each sentence below, there is a comma split. All of the commas in each sentence and the lines below them are numbered. Identify the comma split and write its number in the space next to the sentence number. On the lines under each, write what the comma is splitting on the appropriate line. For the correctly placed commas, write the comma rule "buzzword" on the numbered line. For quotation marks, write *quotation marks*. Since each pair of quotation marks only counts as one thing, there will only be a number under the first quotation mark.

__2__ 7) On Friday, Juan looked at the three, dollars in his hand and said, "That doesn't look like
                1   2   3 4

very much!"

#1 _introductory element_

#2 _splits noun and adjective_

#3 _gear-change comma_

#4 _quotation marks_

__4__ 8) "That's true," said Dad, "but at the end of the month, you'll have, twelve dollars to spend."
           1   2 3   4

#1 _quotation marks_

#2 _gear-change comma_

#3 _quotation marks_

#4 _splits verb and direct object_

__1__ 9) Juan, stared at the money in his hand and said, "Dad, just think of how much I'll have at
             1   2 3 4

the end of the YEAR!"

#1 _splits subject and verb_

#2 _gear-change comma_

#3 _quotation marks_

#4 _direct address_

Direct Quotations: Exercise C

Directions
In this activity, put in all of the correct punctuation needed, including quotation marks, and capitalize where needed. Read each of the following sentences carefully and insert punctuation where it should go. Look back at the lesson notes if you need help.

1) Six months after they had started the program, Juan said to Jason, "I have almost twenty dollars to spend on Craig's birthday present."

2) "Wow!" exclaimed Jason. "How'd you manage that?"

3) "Remember how my parents and I started my savings program?" asked Juan. "I've got the money all saved up."

4) "And another neat thing," Juan added, "is that by the end of the year, I'll have over seventy dollars in my college account."

5) Jason said, "My parents say that as I get older, my chores will increase and so will the money I earn, so both of my savings accounts will grow even faster."

Directions
Edit the following sentences, using the editing marks you have learned. There are five errors. (Because quotation marks always come in pairs, missing quotation marks count as one error, but make sure that you put in both sets.)

6) Juan's grandfather would always give him a ten dollar bill whenever he came for a visit. He would always say, "Juan, remember that money doesn't grow on trees." Juan was proud when he told his grandfather what he was learning about money.

EXERCISE C **8**

Directions
In each sentence below, there is a comma split. All of the commas in each sentence and the lines below them are numbered. Identify the comma split and write its number in the space next to the sentence number. On the lines under each, write what the comma is splitting on the appropriate line. For the correctly placed commas, write the comma rule "buzzword" on the numbered line. For quotation marks, write *quotation marks*. Since each pair of quotation marks only counts as one thing, there will only be a number under the first quotation mark.

__3__ **7)** Juan's grandfather lives in Madison, Wisconsin, and he only gets to visit every six,
                                                         1   2   3
months or so.

#1 _names, dates, & places_

#2 _compound sentence_

#3 _splits noun and adjective_

__1__ **8)** His grandfather's name, is Juan Albert Contreras Sr, and Juan's dad is named after him.
                                        1   2

#1 _splits subject and verb_

#2 _compound sentence_

__1__ **9)** Juan's dad is, Juan Albert Contreras Jr., and, of course, Juan is Juan Albert Contreras III.
                         1   2   3   4

#1 _splits linking verb and complement_

#2 _compound sentence_

#3 _expression_

#4 _expression_

8 ASSESSMENT

Direct Quotations: Assessment

Directions

In this activity, put in all of the correct punctuation needed, including quotation marks, and capitalize where needed. Read each of the following sentences carefully and insert punctuation where it should go. Look back at the lesson notes if you need help.

Each correct punctuation is worth one point. Remember quotation marks count as one error.

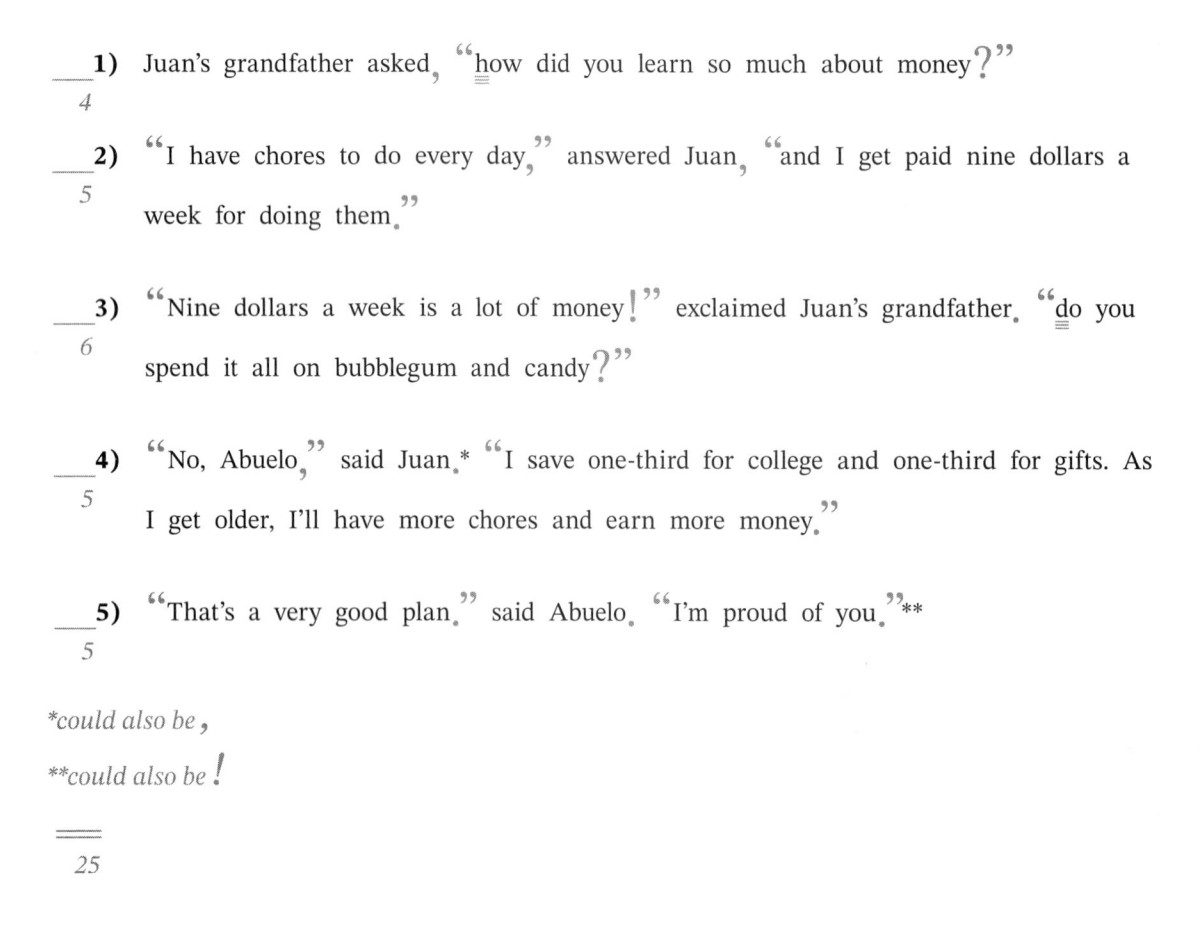

__4__ 1) Juan's grandfather asked, "how did you learn so much about money?"

__5__ 2) "I have chores to do every day," answered Juan, "and I get paid nine dollars a week for doing them."

__6__ 3) "Nine dollars a week is a lot of money!" exclaimed Juan's grandfather. "do you spend it all on bubblegum and candy?"

__5__ 4) "No, Abuelo," said Juan.* "I save one-third for college and one-third for gifts. As I get older, I'll have more chores and earn more money."

__5__ 5) "That's a very good plan." said Abuelo. "I'm proud of you."**

*could also be ,

**could also be !

__25__

Directions

Correct the errors in the following sentences using the editing marks you have learned. There are five errors. Look at the lesson notes if you need help.

Each corrected error is worth one point.

6) "Juan, you've really learned a lot about money," said Abuelo. During Abuelo's visit, Juan had done his chores, received his money, and added to his savings accounts. His grandfather was extremely proud of Juan.

__5__

Assessment 8

Directions

In each sentence below, there is a comma split. All of the commas in each sentence and the lines below them are numbered. Identify the comma split and write its number in the space next to the sentence number. On the lines under each, write what the comma is splitting on the appropriate line. For the correctly placed commas, write the comma rule "buzzword" on the numbered line. For quotation marks, write *quotation marks*. Since each pair of quotation marks only counts as one thing, there will only be a number under the first quotation mark.

Identifying the comma split is worth two points. Identifying what is split and which comma buzzwords apply is worth one point each.

_1_/2 **7)** Money, knowledge should be a part of every student's education, or they might make
                    1   2
expensive mistakes later in life.

    _#1_/1 *splits noun and adjective*

    _#2_/1 *compound sentence*

_3_/2 **8)** "Dad, I've decided that I will always save, a percentage of the money I make," said Juan.
        1 2   3   4

    _#1_/1 *quotation marks*

    _#2_/1 *direct address*

    _#3_/1 *splits verb and direct object*

    _#4_/1 *gear-change comma*

_3_/2 **9)** In a special piggy bank in his room, Juan kept his college savings, and he kept his
                                        1   2
gift savings in a leather, wallet in his dresser.
                           3

    _#1_/1 *introductory element*

    _#2_/1 *compound sentence*

    _#3_/1 *splits noun and adjective*

15

Total Points 54 $\dfrac{43}{54} = 80\%$

Lesson 9
Titles

Lesson 9: Titles

The buzzword for this rule is *titles*.

Books, magazines, plays, movies, and many other things have *titles*. Did you ever read *Goodnight Moon* or *Hop on Pop* when you were little? When we use the titles of things in sentences, we underline, italicize, or use quotation marks to show that we are talking about a title. We also capitalize them differently. If we don't do these things, our writing can be confusing.

Imagine a book about furniture called *The Living Room*. Now read the following sentence:

> I was reading yesterday in the living room that red couches are popular.

Are you talking about the book, or were you actually in the living room while you were reading? There's no way to tell! That's why it's important to be clear:

> I was reading yesterday in *The Living Room* that red couches are popular.

The way to know what to underline or italicize and what to put in quotation marks has to do with *size*. Look at the following chart:

Underline or *Italicize*	Put in "Quotation Marks"
books	chapters
newspapers	newspaper articles
CDs or albums	songs
movies	TV or radio shows
plays	poems
magazines	magazine articles

Compare the items on the left to the ones on the right. You will see that **major**, or **larger**, works get underlined/italicized, while **minor**, or **smaller** works get quotation marks.

Examples: In *USA Today* there was an article called "The Schooling Game" that talked about different schools around the country.

Have you read the chapter called "The Piano Lesson" in that book *How to Be a Musician*?

How do you know which words should be capitalized in a title? Here are a few guidelines.

- **Capitalize** all nouns, pronouns, adjectives, verbs, and adverbs.
- **Do not capitalize** articles, prepositions, or coordinating conjunctions (FANBOYS).
- **Always capitalize** the first and last words of the title, no matter what kind of words they are.

> Titles in quotation marks should usually not be set apart from the rest of the sentence with commas. If the title comes at the end of the sentence, though, make sure that the ending punctuation mark is inside the closing quotation mark!

The examples shown here are *italicized* because this book is printed. If you are typing on a computer, use *italics*. But if you're writing by hand and you mention a major work, what do you do when you can't italicize? That's when you will underline. Both underlining and *italicizing* show the same thing—that the title refers to a major work.

Titles: Exercise A

Directions
In the sentences below, there are certain titles. Put quotation marks around the ones that need quotation marks and underline the ones that need to be underlined.

1) My book <u>Adventures in Neverland</u> was due back to the library.

2) When I went to the library to return it, the librarian was reading a story called "How To* Say No to a Monster."

> *Why is this *to* capitalized? The answer is that it's not a preposition. Remember that a word is only a preposition when it is used in a prepositional phrase. This *To* is doing a different job than the *to* in the prepositional phrase *to a monster*.

3) After the story, she read one of my favorite poems called "Jabberwocky."

4) Then, after choosing different parts to act, we read a play called <u>Anne Meets Gilbert</u>.

5) Finally, we heard a new CD by Kermit the Frog called <u>Being Nice to Green Things</u>.

Directions
Edit the following sentences, using the editing marks you have learned. There are five errors. Look back at your notes if you need help.

6) Well, I just love to go to the library! Our local one is at 425 Elm Street, Middleborough, Ohio. My idea for a great day is to check out a stack of books, take them home to my room, and read through them one after another. In a cozy corner of my bedroom, there's a comfortable chair that's my favorite spot for reading.

9 EXERCISE A

Directions
In each sentence below there is a comma split. All of the commas in each sentence and the lines below them are numbered. Identify the comma split and write its number in the space next to the sentence number. On the lines under each, write what the comma is splitting on the appropriate line. On the other lines, write the "buzzword" for that punctuation rule. Remember that each pair of quotation marks only counts as one thing. There is a number under the open quote mark or the entire title, but there is not one under the close quote mark.

__1__ 7) The lady at our local library, always says, "Remember to keep your voice down!"
            1   2 3

#1 _splits subject and verb_

#2 _gear change comma_

#3 _quotation marks_

__2__ 8) During my trip to the library, I usually pick, one thrilling, spine-tingling mystery book.
                1   2   3

#1 _introductory element_

#2 _splits verb and direct object_

#3 _two adjectives tests_

__1__ 9) The latest mystery book I read was, The Case of the Hidden Birdcage, and I read it all
                                  1   2   3

in one afternoon!

#1 _splits linking verb and complement_

#2 _titles_

#3 _compound sentence_

Titles: Exercise B

Directions
In the sentences below, there are certain titles. Put quotation marks around the ones that need quotation marks and underline the ones that need to be underlined.

1) Last Saturday, my buddies and I went to see the new movie <u>The New Adventures of the Hulk</u>.

2) It is based on the story "Hulk Strikes Again."

3) You can find that story in the magazine <u>Everyday Superheroes</u>.

4) After the movie, we were all singing the theme song "Hulk Saves the Day."

5) I'm going to buy the CD called <u>Songs for Superheroes</u>.

Directions
Edit the following sentences, using the editing marks you have learned. There are five errors. Look back at your notes if you need help.

6) My mom said, "Kevin, you've been singing that song all day. It's driving me nuts!" I gave my mom, an apologetic look and told her that I'd really try to stop. With a huge effort on my part, I managed to stop singing the song for about fifteen minutes, but then it just, popped out of my mouth!

9 EXERCISE B

Directions
In each sentence below there is a comma split. All of the commas in each sentence and the lines below them are numbered. Identify the comma split and write its number in the space next to the sentence number. On the lines under each, write what the comma is splitting on the appropriate line. On the other lines, write the "buzzword" for that punctuation rule. Remember that each pair of quotation marks only counts as one thing. There is a number under the open quote mark or the entire title, but there is not one under the close quote mark.

__1__ 7) Kevin loves to pretend that he is, a superhero, but his little sister Marie loves beautiful,
                                      1   2   3

exotic animals.

#1 _splits linking verb and complement_

#2 _compound sentence_

#3 _two adjectives tests_

__1__ 8) Marie has a CD called Let's Sing about Animals with all her favorite, songs about capybaras,
                                                                          1   2

gnus, and cheetahs.
  3

#1 _splits noun and adjective_

#2 _items in a series_

#3 _items in a series_

__2__ 9) Marie and Kevin have different interests, but they have their best, times together with a
                                                 1   2

couple of old cardboard boxes!

#1 _compound sentence_

#2 _splits noun and adjective_

Titles: Exercise C

Directions
In the sentences below, there are certain titles. Put quotation marks around the ones that need quotation marks and underline the ones that need to be underlined.

1) Last Saturday afternoon, I decided to re-read my favorite book, <u>Mrs. Piggle-Wiggle</u>.

2) My favorite story in that book is called "The Selfishness Cure."

3) Then I read one of my favorite poems called "Casey at the Bat."

4) That poem gave me the idea to read the sports section of our local newspaper the <u>Morning Call</u>.

5) Reading about last night's baseball game made me feel like singing the old song "Take Me Out to the Ballgame."

Directions
Edit the following sentences, using the editing marks you have learned. There are five errors. Look back at your notes if you need help.

6) My uncle, James Patterson Wilson, Jr., played minor league baseball when he was a young man. He was the star pitcher, as a matter of fact, of the Danville Devils. He loves to tell the story of the time he hit the winning home run in the final game of the series. Yes, he will remember that day always!

9 EXERCISE C

Directions
In each sentence below there is a comma split. All of the commas in each sentence and the lines below them are numbered. Identify the comma split and write its number in the space next to the sentence number. On the lines under each, write what the comma is splitting on the appropriate line. On the other lines, write the "buzzword" for that punctuation rule. Remember that each pair of quotation marks only counts as one thing. There is a number under the open quote mark or the entire title, but there is not one under the close quote mark.

__2__ 7) The poem "Casey at the Bat" is about the last, inning of a baseball game with two outs, two
                    1   2   3
strikes, and bases loaded.
        4

#1 _quotation marks_

#2 _splits noun and adjective_

#3 _items in a series_

#4 _items in a series_

__2__ 8) Proud, arrogant Casey, walked slowly up to the plate to take his turn at bat.
              1   2

#1 _two adjectives tests_

#2 _splits subject and verb_

__1__ 9) Everything, depended on Casey's getting a hit, but you must read the poem to find out
                       1   2
what happened!

#1 _splits subject and verb_

#2 _compound sentence_

Titles: Assessment

Directions

In the sentences below, there are certain titles. Put quotation marks around the ones that need quotation marks and underline the ones that need to be underlined.

Each correct punctuation is worth one point. Remember quotation marks count as one error.

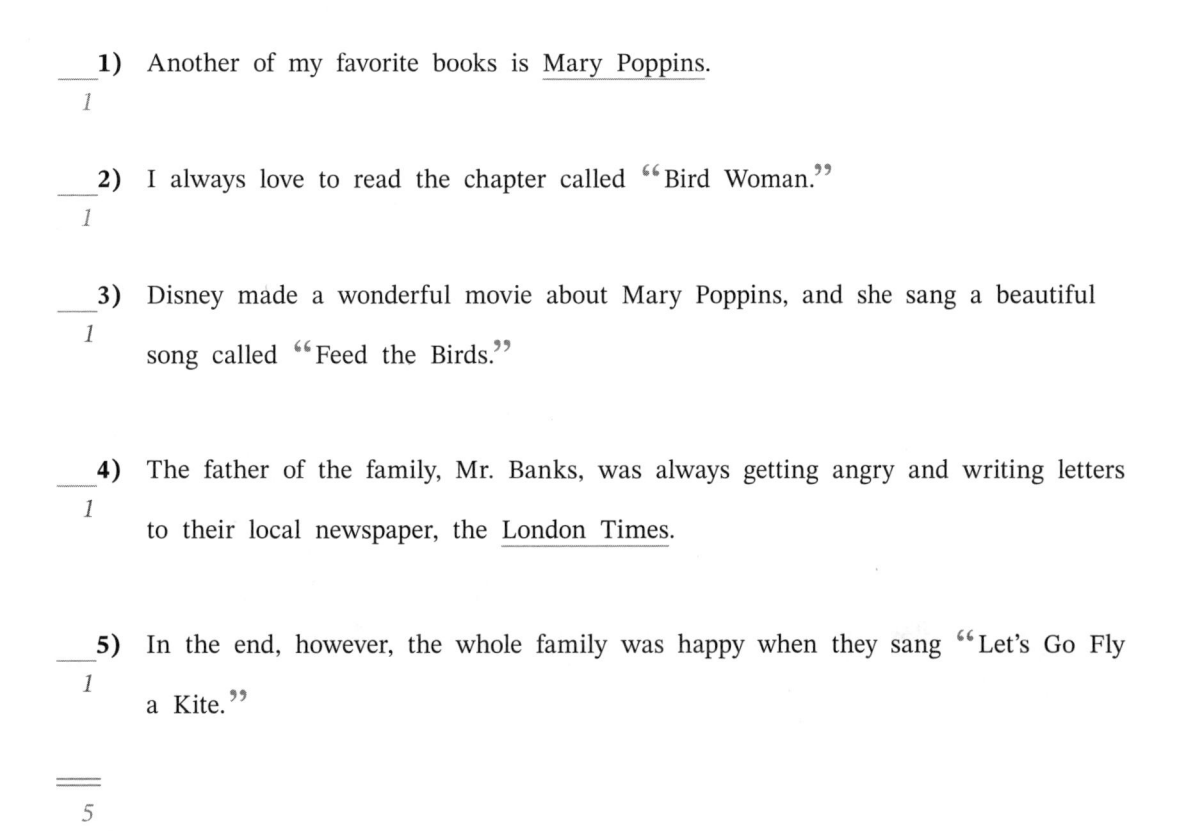

   __1__ 1) Another of my favorite books is <u>Mary Poppins</u>.

   __1__ 2) I always love to read the chapter called "Bird Woman."

   __1__ 3) Disney made a wonderful movie about Mary Poppins, and she sang a beautiful song called "Feed the Birds."

   __1__ 4) The father of the family, Mr. Banks, was always getting angry and writing letters to their local newspaper, the <u>London Times</u>.

   __1__ 5) In the end, however, the whole family was happy when they sang "Let's Go Fly a Kite."

   ==5==

Directions

Edit the following sentences, using the editing marks you have learned. There are five errors. Look back at your notes if you need help.

Each corrected error is worth one point.

6) In the book called <u>Mary Poppins</u>, the Banks family consisted of Mr. and Mrs. Banks, Jane, Michael, and twin babies. They advertised for a new nanny to work at their house at 2 Cherry Tree Lane, London, England. After she said firmly, "I make it a rule never to give references," Mary Poppins slid up the banister! Jane and Michael knew that this nanny was someone very special.

   ==5==

9 ASSESSMENT

Directions

In each sentence below there is a comma split. All of the commas in each sentence and the lines below them are numbered. Identify the comma split and write its number in the space next to the sentence number. On the lines under each, write what the comma is splitting on the appropriate line. On the other lines, write the "buzzword" for that punctuation rule. Remember that each pair of quotation marks only counts as one thing. There is a number under the open quote mark or the entire title, but there is not one under the close quote mark.

Identifying the comma split is worth two points. Identifying what is split and which comma buzzwords apply is worth one point each.

__2__ / 2 7) On the day of their first outing, Mary Poppins, took Jane and Michael to visit Uncle
                                                        1   2

Albert in a chapter called "Laughing Gas."
                              3

__1__ #1 *introductory element*

__1__ #2 *splits subject and verb*

__1__ #3 *titles*

__2__ / 2 8) Well, Uncle Albert, was a round, jolly old man who was floating in the air in his parlor
                     1   2   3

because it was his birthday.

__1__ #1 *introductory element*

__1__ #2 *splits subject and verb*

__1__ #3 *two adjectives tests*

__2__ / 2 9) "When I laugh on that particular, day I become so filled with laughing gas that I
               1   2

simply can't keep on the ground," said Uncle Albert.
                                     3

__ /1 #1 *quotation marks*

__ /1 #2 *splits noun and adjective*

__ /1 #3 *ear change comma*

15

Total Points $\dfrac{20}{25}$ = 80%

Lesson 10
Possessives

Lesson 10: Possessives

The buzzword for this lesson is *possessives*.

Think of your most treasured possession. Is it a toy? A trophy? A book? A family heirloom? There is a little girl named Maddie, and her prized possession is her stuffed koala.

> Maddie has a stuffed koala in her room.

Can you think of a way to say that the koala belongs to Maddie? How about:

> Maddie's stuffed koala is in her room.

We turned *Maddie* into a **possessive adjective** (usually just called a **possessive**) by adding an apostrophe followed by *s* to the end: *Maddie's*. Now we know who the koala belongs to.

The first rule of making possessives is this:

> **Add 's to a singular noun.**

If there's only one of a noun (a singular noun, like *cat* or *house*, for example), add *'s*. This is true **no matter what letter the singular noun ends with.** Here are some other examples of singular nouns that have been made into possessive adjectives by adding *'s*:

> The brown dog's bark was the loudest.
>
> My aunt's apple pie is the best!
>
> Our home's porch needs a coat of paint.
>
> We admired the bass's stripes before we threw it back.

> **Be careful! Never use 's to make something plural!**
>
> We use plurals when we mean more than one of something. We use possessives to show ownership of something. They're very different, so we need to make sure we don't get them mixed up. This is a great way to quietly show your grammar knowledge, because many people struggle with knowing the difference.

The second rule of making possessives is this:

> **Add an apostrophe (') to a plural noun that *already ends in -s*. Add 's to plural nouns that *do not end in -s*.**

Most plural nouns already end in *-s*. Rather than adding another *'s*, simply add an apostrophe (') after the ending *-s*.

> **Examples:** The brown dogs' barks were the loudest. (*more than one dog = dogs*)
>
> My aunts' apple pies are the best! (*more than one aunt = aunts*)
>
> The homes' porches need a coat of paint. (*more than one home = homes*)
>
> We admired the basses' stripes before we threw them back. (*more than one bass = basses**)

*The plural of bass *can also be* bass. *Either is correct. The possessive form of* bass *(plural) is* bass'.

But some plural nouns don't end in -s. To show possession, they need 's added.

belonging to the children = *children's*

belonging to the sheep = *sheep's*

belonging to the oxen = *oxen's*

Singular	Singular Possessive	Plural	Plural Possessive
dog	dog's	dogs	dogs'
aunt	aunt's	aunts	aunts'
child	child's	children	children's
bass	bass's	basses (*or* bass)	basses' (*or* bass')
ox	ox's	oxen	oxen's
sheep	sheep's	sheep	sheep's*

Sheep is a tricky one! With nouns like *sheep*, you really need to read the sentence for context to know how many there are.

There's one more kind of possessive adjective to know about. Look back at this example sentence:

Maddie's stuffed koala is in her room.

We know *Maddie's* is a possessive. There's another possessive in that sentence, too. Can you find it? It is the possessive adjective *her*. *My, her, his, its, their,* and *your* are pronouns that show possession. If you were labeling the parts of speech in a sentence, you would mark them as adjectives, but they are usually called **possessive pronouns**. They are already possessive, so they **do not need 's.**

Here is another piece of grammar that is very often confused: ***it's*** vs. ***its***.

It's is a contraction of **it is**.   **Its** is a possessive pronoun meaning **belonging to it**.

Remember that **possessive pronouns never get 's**. If you are writing a sentence and aren't sure whether you should use ***it's*** or ***its***, try substituting ***it is*** in your sentence:

The kitten has lost ***it's/its*** mittens.

Test: The kitten has lost ***it is*** mittens.

Well, that makes no sense, does it? The mittens belong to the kitten—they belong to ***it***. Use the possessive pronoun ***its*** with **no apostrophe**.

Correct: The kitten has lost ***its*** mittens.

It's/Its going to look for them.

Test: ***It is*** going to look for them.

Perfect! Use the contraction ***it's*** in this sentence.

Correct: ***It's*** going to look for them.

10 EXERCISE A

Possessives: Exercise A

Directions
Read the sentences carefully and decide if there is a plural or a possessive in the underlined phrase. Write **PL** in the blank if it's **plural** and **PO** if it should be **possessive**. But *be careful*: We have left the apostrophes off of the possessives on purpose!

<u>PL</u>   1) <u>The boys in my neighborhood</u> played basketball after school.

<u>PO</u>   2) <u>My friends basketball</u> was in the best condition.

<u>PO</u>   3) They all played in <u>Jasons driveway</u> because it was the biggest.

<u>PL</u>   4) They organized themselves into teams of <u>four players each</u>.

<u>PO</u>   5) After a hard-fought game, <u>the older players team</u> was the winner!

Directions
Some of the sentences below need **plurals**, and some need **possessives**. Circle the correct word. Remember that plurals do not have apostrophes. Look back at your notes if you need help.

6) After their defeat, the younger (**(boys)**, boy's) decided they wanted a rematch.

7) We decided to practice in my (neighbors, **(neighbor's)**) driveway.

8) All the (**(neighbors)**, neighbor's) got excited about the rematch.

9) My best (friends, **(friend's)**) excellent shooting ability was a big plus!

10) Even the (**(parents)**, parent's) on the street started to get in on the fun.

Exercise A 10

Directions

In each sentence below there is a comma split. All of the commas in each sentence and the lines below them are numbered. Identify the comma split and write its number in the space next to the sentence number. On the lines under each, write what the comma is splitting on the appropriate line. On the other lines, write the "buzzword" for that punctuation rule. Remember that each pair of quotation marks only counts as one thing. There is a number under the open quote mark or the entire title, but there is not one under the close quote mark.

__2__ 11) Good, vigorous exercise, is one of the most important ways to keep our bodies healthy, but
             1   2   3

we often get lazy.

#1 _two adjectives tests_

#2 _splits subject and verb_

#3 _compound sentence_

__3__ 12) In my latest <u>Highlights</u> magazine, the whole, theme was about exercise, games, and health.
                           1   2   3   4   5

#1 _titles_

#2 _introductory element_

#3 _splits noun and adjective_

#4 _items in a series_

#5 _items in a series_

__1__ 13) One writer wrote, a story about a boy's decision to get up off the couch and get daily exercise.
                         1   2

#1 _splits verb and direct object_

#2 _possessives_

10 Exercise B

Possessives: Exercise B

Directions
Some of the sentences below need **plurals** and some need **possessives**. Circle the correct word. Remember that plurals do not have apostrophes. Look back at the lesson notes if you need help.

1) One (girls, (girl's)) favorite form of exercise is her ballet class.

2) If you watch ((dancers,) dancer's) on television, you can see that they are in top physical condition.

3) My other (friends, (friend's)) dance class includes ballet, jazz, and tap.

Directions
All of the sentences below contain possessives. Put the apostrophe (') in the correct place.

4) The ballet teacher's name is Miss Cindy.

5) She studied ballet at New York's famous Juilliard School of Music.

6) Miss Cindy's plan was to be a ballerina, but she decided to teach instead.

Directions
Edit the following sentences using the editing marks you have learned. There are five errors (but remember: quotation marks only count as one thing, even if both sets are missing!). Look back at your notes if you need help.

7) Dad said, "Let's walk to the park today and get some exercise!" We were all excited about going to the park, and we got our play clothes and running shoes on. I was determined to try out some new stretching exercises I saw in a story called "Get Your Body Ready" from my latest *Running* magazine. I was sure I looked like a real athlete in my new shoes and gear!

EXERCISE B 10

Directions
In each sentence below there is a comma split. All of the commas in each sentence and the lines below them are numbered. Identify the comma split and write its number in the space next to the sentence number. On the lines under each, write what the comma is splitting on the appropriate line. On the other lines, write the "buzzword" for that punctuation rule. Remember that each pair of quotation marks only counts as one thing. There is a number under the open quote mark or the entire title, but there is not one under the close quote mark.

__2__ 8) At the beginning of vigorous exercise, it is a good idea to stretch the muscles gently to avoid
                                              1
any, injury.
  2

#1 _introductory element_

#2 _splits noun and adjective_

__3__ 9) Young children, on the other hand, do not need to stretch, their muscles when they go
                    1   2   3
out to play.

#1 _expressions_

#2 _expressions_

#3 _splits verb and direct object_

__2__ 10) My young friend, be sure to include, some exercise in your day, or your body will grow weak.
                          1   2   3

#1 _direct address_

#2 _splits verb and direct object_

#3 _compound sentence_

10 EXERCISE C

Possessives: Exercise C

Directions
All the sentences below include possessives. Put the apostrophes (') in the correct place. Look back at the lesson notes if you need help.

1) All my body's muscles are designed to do certain jobs.

2) My mom's advice to me is always to get up and get moving.

3) On the weekends, my dad's idea is to get us involved in some physical game.

4) I usually try to overcome my big brother's height advantage by being quick.

5) My big sister's strategy is to yell as much as possible!

Directions
Edit the following sentences using the editing marks you have learned. There are five errors. Look back at your notes if you need help.

6) Our house at 220 Elm Avenue, Elm Forest, Illinois, is usually the place where everybody gathers to play. Our big, beautiful back yard, is perfect for running around. My dad said, "Jimmy, let's think of a game where your sister's loud voice has to be quiet!" Our brilliant, idea was to organize a game of hide and seek.

EXERCISE C **10**

Directions

In each sentence below there is a comma split. All of the commas in each sentence and the lines below them are numbered. Identify the comma split and write its number in the space next to the sentence number. On the lines under each, write what the comma is splitting on the appropriate line. On the other lines, write the "buzzword" for that punctuation rule. Remember that each pair of quotation marks only counts as one thing. There is a number under the open quote mark or the entire title, but there is not one under the close quote mark.

_3_ 7) At the start of the game, my brother's deep voice, could be heard counting, "one...
                          1   2   3   4

two... three..."

#1 _introductory element_

#2 _possessives_

#3 _splits subject and verb_

#4 _quotation marks_

_3_ 8) My dad, my sister, and I all hid in different, places in the yard.
              1   2   3

#1 _items in a series_

#2 _items in a series_

#3 _splits noun and modifier_

_3_ 9) Well, I hid behind my mom's big azalea bush, and my brother gave me, a big grin when he
         1   2   3

found me.

#1 _introductory element_

#2 _compound sentence_

#3 _splits indirect object and direct object_

INSTRUCTOR HANDBOOK   ANALYTICAL GRAMMAR: LEVEL 2 - MECHANICS • LESSON 10 • EXERCISE C **97**

10 ASSESSMENT

Possessives: Assessment

Directions
All of the sentences below contain possessives. Put the apostrophe (') in the correct place. Be sure to read carefully to find all of the possessives in the sentence. Look back at the lesson notes if you need help.

Each correctly placed apostrophe is worth one point.

__1__ 1) One of my neighborhood's big traditions is to have an organized field day each spring.

__1__ 2) My dad's favorite event is the tug o' war.

__2__ 3) The three-legged race is my favorite, when my mom's leg is tied to my sister's leg and they race together.

__2__ 4) My best friend's best event is the sack race, when he hops to the finish line in one of Mr. Parker's feed sacks.

__2__ 5) Everybody's input is required to make our field day a success, even though some folks prefer not to compete and just sit in my mom's lawn chairs.

__8__

Directions
Edit the following sentences using the editing marks you have learned. There are five errors. Look back at your notes if you need help.

Each corrected error is worth one point.

6) At the end of the day, we all gather together for a big hamburger and hotdog cookout. "Jason, you're in charge of everybody's drinks," said Dad. All the neighbors bring food, and the grownups talk while we kids play. My next-door neighbor's potato salad is always the biggest hit.

__5__

98 ANALYTICAL GRAMMAR: LEVEL 2 - MECHANICS • LESSON 10 • ASSESSMENT   INSTRUCTOR HANDBOOK

ASSESSMENT 10

Directions

In each sentence below there is a comma split. All of the commas in each sentence and the lines below them are numbered. Identify the comma split and write its number in the space next to the sentence number. On the lines under each, write what the comma is splitting on the appropriate line. On the other lines, write the "buzzword" for that punctuation rule. Remember that each pair of quotation marks only counts as one thing. There is a number under the open quote mark or the entire title, but there is not one under the close quote mark.

Identifying the comma split is worth two points. Identifying what is split and which comma buzzwords apply is worth one point each.

__2__ 7) As a matter of fact, our, neighborhood's next field day is scheduled for Saturday,
_2_   1   2   3
July 14, 2022.
         4

__1__ #1 _expressions (or introductory element)_
__1__ #2 _splits noun and modifier_
__1__ #3 _names, dates, & places_
__1__ #4 _names, dates, & places_

__1__ 8) I, hope it will be a gorgeous, sunny day for the event, or we'll have to do it indoors.
_2_   1   2   3

__1__ #1 _splits subject and verb_
__1__ #2 _two adjectives tests_
__1__ #3 _compound sentence_

__5__ 9) "Jason, we need to start exercising to get ready for next year's tug o' war, " Dad, said.
_2_   1   2   3   4   5

__1__ #1 _quotation marks_
__1__ #2 _direct address_
__1__ #3 _possessives_
__1__ #4 _gear change comma_
__1__ #5 _splits subject and verb_

==
18

=== *Total Points* $\dfrac{25}{31} = 80\%$
31

INSTRUCTOR HANDBOOK   ANALYTICAL GRAMMAR: LEVEL 2 - MECHANICS • LESSON 10 • ASSESSMENT 99

Lesson 11
Capitalization

Lesson 11: Capitalization

The buzzword for this lesson is *capitalize*.

my friend sarah goes to crabtree valley mall every sunday.

Does the sentence above look a little weird? Yes! And you can quickly see why, right? Nothing is capitalized like it should be! How should this look?

My friend Sarah goes to Crabtree Valley Mall every Sunday.

That's more like it. Capital letters are used to signal to readers that a new sentence has begun or that what they're reading is the proper name of something. You probably already know that you need to capitalize the first letter of a new sentence. You most likely capitalize your name, too. So you're already ahead of the game!

> There are two editing symbols that are used to correct letters that should or should not be capitalized. You'll use these symbols in your editing practice in the lesson exercises. You've already seen the first one in Lesson 8.
>
> To show that a letter should be uppercase, draw three little lines under it:
>
> United states
>
> To show that a letter should be lowercase, draw a line through it:
>
> the blue Car

There are different reasons that we capitalize words, so we've provided examples of each.

A) Capitalize the names of people, places, and things. If a person has a title, capitalize that, too, if it comes before their name. Remember, these are called proper nouns.

    People: Maria, Mr. Spencer, President Kennedy, Great-Aunt Toby

    Places: Italy, the Sistine Chapel, Indiana University, Main Street, Hawaii

    Things: the Hope Diamond, the Empire State Building, Thanksgiving

B) Capitalize proper adjectives. If you make an adjective out of a proper noun, capitalize it.

    Greek theater, Mr. Spencer's shoes, Italian meal, Indiana University basketball

C) Capitalize the brand names of products.

Generic Name (don't capitalize)	Brand Name (capitalize)
math program	Math-U-See®
spelling program	Spelling You See®
company	Demme Learning®

D) Capitalize all the words in the titles of books, songs, news articles, etc., **except** prepositions, articles, and conjunctions. You've already learned this in Lesson 9.

    A Wrinkle in Time   *The One and Only Ivan*

    My Side of the Mountain   "Running the Right Way"

E) Capitalize the names of races, ethnicities, nationalities, and religions.

Races and ethnicities: Indian, Asian, Black, Irish-American

Nationalities: American, European, Israeli, Greek

Religions: Catholic, Buddhist, Seventh-Day Adventist

F) Capitalize the days of the week and the months of the year.

Monday, January, March, Tuesday

11 EXERCISE A

Capitalization: Exercise A

Directions
Mark the letters in the sentences below that should be capitalized by drawing three short lines beneath the letter, as shown in the lesson notes. Mark the letters that are capitalized but should not be with a diagonal line through the letter. Look back at the lesson notes if you need help remembering any of the rules. Watch out for those proper adjectives (adjectives made from proper nouns). They're sneaky!

1) I just got ~~B~~ack from a trip to smoky mountain national park.

2) it was a field trip for our sunday school class at first baptist church in richmond, virginia.

3) I shared a ~~T~~ent with my buddies juan, dal, and mason.

4) our teacher mr. james greene showed ~~U~~s how to survive in the wild.

5) it was fun when our group met up with a bunch of guys from a catholic church group who were also camping.

Directions
Edit the following sentences using the editing marks you have learned. If you find a letter that needs to be capitalized, draw three short lines beneath it. There are seven errors. Look back at your notes if you need help.

6) One of the boys in our group, dal, just moved here from the city. He has never used, a fishing pole in his life. Mr. greene showed Dal how to hold the pole and what to do. As soon as he put it in the water, Dal's pole dipped strongly. "Dal, pull up your pole!" shouted Mr. Greene. Dal was, amazed when he pulled up a beautiful, big fish!

EXERCISE A **11**

Directions

In each sentence below there is a comma split. All of the commas in each sentence and the lines below them are numbered. Identify the comma split and write its number in the space next to the sentence number. On the lines under each, write what the comma is splitting on the appropriate line. On the other lines, write the "buzzword" for that punctuation rule. Remember that each pair of quotation marks only counts as one thing. There is a number under the open quote mark or the entire title, but there is not one under the close quote mark.

_2_ 7) Mr. Greene showed, Dal how to clean his fish, and we had a big, delicious fish fry for dinner.
                       1   2   3   4

    #1 _capitalize_

    #2 _splits verb and direct object_

    #3 _compound sentence_

    #4 _two adjectives tests_

_2_ 8) At the end of dinner, we, celebrated Dal's triumph by singing "For He's a Jolly Good Fellow."
                                    1 2   3   4

    #1 _introductory element_

    #2 _splits subject and verb_

    #3 _possessives_

    #4 _titles_

_1_ 9) Mr. Greene told us, some stories, and we spent the rest of the evening singing around
                                     1   2

the campfire.

    #1 _splits indirect object and direct object_

    #2 _compound sentence_

11 EXERCISE B

Capitalization: Exercise B

Directions
Mark the letters in the sentences below that should be capitalized by drawing three short lines beneath the letter. Mark the letters that are capitalized but should not be with a diagonal line through the letter. Look back at the lesson notes if you need help. Watch out for those proper adjectives—they're sneaky!

1) One day on our trip, we made arrangements to ℂamp with a group of kids from a jewish community center in new york city.

2) Their leader was mr. jerome steinberg, and he and Øur mr. greene had been roommates at penn state university.

3) we had a great time around the campfire that night as mr. greene and mr. steinberg told stories about their crazy college days.

4) Then mr. steinberg read us a Ṣcary Ṣtory called "the gold bug."

5) It was a little creepy as we sat under the shadow of the great smoky mountains.

Directions
Edit the following sentences using the editing marks you have learned. If you find a letter that needs to be capitalized, draw three short lines beneath it. There are eight errors.

6) At the end of the story, the two leaders said, "it's time to turn in, guys!" We headed toward our neatly pitched/ tent and crawled into our warm sleeping bags. After some whispering, giggling, and joking, Mr. greene told us it was/ time to go to sleep.

Exercise B 11

Directions

In each sentence below there is a comma split. All of the commas in each sentence and the lines below them are numbered. Identify the comma split and write its number in the space next to the sentence number. On the lines under each, write what the comma is splitting on the appropriate line. On the other lines, write the "buzzword" for that punctuation rule. Remember that each pair of quotation marks only counts as one thing. There is a number under the open quote mark or the entire title, but there is not one under the close quote mark.

__3__ 7) We awoke to a cool, misty morning, and we decided that we, should spend the day looking
                                          1   2   3

for huckleberries.

- #1 _two adjectives tests_
- #2 _compound sentence_
- #3 _splits subject and verb_

__3__ 8) After all, Mr. Steinberg was an expert at spotting ripe, delicious, huckleberries in the woods.
                    1   2   3

- #1 _introductory element (or expressions)_
- #2 _two adjectives tests_
- #3 _splits noun and adjective_

__3__ 9) Mr. Steinberg's son, Jerome Steinberg Jr., got the most huckleberries, and he got to choose
                          1   2

at which meal we, would eat them!
                  3

- #1 _possessives_
- #2 _compound sentence_
- #3 _splits subject and verb_

11 EXERCISE C

Capitalization: Exercise C

Directions
Mark the letters in the sentences below that should be capitalized by drawing three short lines beneath the letter. Mark the letters that are capitalized but should not be with a diagonal line through the letter. Look back at the lesson notes if you need help. Watch out for those proper adjectives—they're sneaky!

1) jerome decided to use a huckleberry pancake recipe from *recipes for the campfire*.

2) juan, dal, mason, and I helped him to make the ~~P~~ancakes.

3) as we worked, we all sang "the bear went over the mountain" at the top of our lungs.

4) Mr. greene, mr. Steinberg, and the rest of the ~~G~~uys declared that our creation "huckleberry morning surprise" was great!

5) We rounded out our ~~B~~reakfast with canadian bacon, florida orange juice, and lots of vermont maple syrup.

Directions
Edit the following sentences using the editing marks you have learned. If you find a letter that needs to be capitalized, draw three short lines beneath it. There are eight errors.

6) After our huge, delicious breakfast, we all pitched in to clean up our campsite. Our plan for the day was to meet up with another group of campers led by one of Mr. Greenes' college buddies named Ken yakamoto. He had a group of kids who live in Tokyo, Japan. Well, we were fascinated to meet and hike with these guys!

EXERCISE C **11**

Directions
In each sentence below there is a comma split. All of the commas in each sentence and the lines below them are numbered. Identify the comma split and write its number in the space next to the sentence number. On the lines under each, write what the comma is splitting on the appropriate line. On the other lines, write the "buzzword" for that punctuation rule. Remember that each pair of quotation marks only counts as one thing. There is a number under the open quote mark or the entire title, but there is not one under the close quote mark.

__4__ 7) Well, I was paired up with a boy named Miko, and this, was his first time camping.
            1   2   3   4

    #1 _introductory element_

    #2 _capitalize_

    #3 _compound sentence_

    #4 _splits subject and verb_

__2__ 8) "I speak, a little English," said Miko in a soft, careful voice.
        1   2   3

    #1 _quotation marks_

    #2 _splits verb and direct object_

    #3 _two adjectives tests_

__2__ 9) Needless to say, I was, extremely relieved, because I don't speak a word of Japanese!
                            1   2   3

    #1 _expressions_

    #2 _splits linking verb and complement_

    #3 _capitalize_

11 ASSESSMENT

Capitalization: Assessment

Directions
Mark the letters in the sentences below that should be capitalized by drawing three short lines beneath the letter. Mark the letters that are capitalized but should not be with a diagonal line through the letter. Look back at the lesson notes if you need help. Watch out for those proper adjectives—they're sneaky!

Each corrected capitalization error is worth one point.

____ 1) we baptists and our jewish and japanese hiking buddies had a great time in smoky mountains national park.
  8

____ 2) Mr. greene, Mr. steinberg, and mr. Yakamoto kept Us from getting lost on the Trails.
  5

____ 3) We really enjoyed our snacks of american cheese, jewish matzo crackers, and japanese noodles.
  3

____ 4) On our last night, we pitched our Tent a little too close to west fork creek, and I soaked my new sleeping bag.
  4

____ 5) We decided that we should all write a book called *camping for non-campers*!
  3

____
 23

Directions
Edit the following sentences using the editing marks you have learned. If you find a letter that needs to be capitalized, draw three short lines beneath it. There are eight errors.

Each corrected error is worth one point.

6) We made, a lot of mistakes on our trip but we had a lot of fun. Our three teachers, on the other hand taught us a lot. After the loss of my sleeping bag they put together a warm dry place for me to sleep. Mr. Greenes book Hiking with Rookies was, a huge help.

____
 8

110 ANALYTICAL GRAMMAR: LEVEL 2 - MECHANICS • LESSON 11 • ASSESSMENT   INSTRUCTOR HANDBOOK

ASSESSMENT 11

Directions

In each sentence below there is a comma split. All of the commas in each sentence and the lines below them are numbered. Identify the comma split and write its number in the space next to the sentence number. On the lines under each, write what the comma is splitting on the appropriate line. On the other lines, write the "buzzword" for that punctuation rule. Remember that each pair of quotation marks only counts as one thing. There is a number under the open quote mark or the entire title, but there is not one under the close quote mark.

Identifying the comma split is worth two points. Identifying what is split and which comma buzzwords apply is worth one point each.

$\underline{4}$ 7) I want to become a pen pal with Miko in Tokyo, Japan, so I got his address and put it
$\overline{2}$ 1   2   3

    in my little, book.
              4

        #1 *capitalize*
      1
        #2 *names, dates, & places*
      1
        #3 *compound sentence*
      1
        #4 *splits noun and adjective*
      1

$\underline{1}$ 8) My family is planning, a trip to Japan, and Miko and I are going to meet on Sunday,
$\overline{2}$ 1   2   3

    May 3, 2022.
         4

        #1 *splits verb and direct object*
      1
        #2 *capitalize*
      1
        #3 *compound sentence*
      1
        #4 *names, dates, & places*
      1

$\underline{1}$ 9) It will be, so much fun to meet Miko's family and eat great Japanese food!
$\overline{2}$ 1   2   3

        #1 *splits linking verb and complement*
      1
        #2 *possessives*
      1
        #3 *capitalize*
      1

$\overline{\overline{17}}$

$\overline{\overline{48}}$ *Total Points* $\dfrac{38}{48} = 80\%$

Lesson 12
Pronoun-Antecedent Agreement

Lesson 12: Pronoun-Antecedent Agreement

The buzzword for this rule is *pronoun-antecedent agreement* (or *pro-ant agr*, since that's a lot easier!).

As a reminder, a *pronoun* takes the place of a noun, and an *antecedent* is a noun a pronoun replaces.

Example: **Jack** said he and **Maria** are going fishing this weekend. (*He is the pronoun and Jack is its antecedent*)

We need to know what the antecedent for a pronoun is, because those two things must agree. That means they must match in **number**, **gender**, and **person**. It doesn't matter if the pronoun is doing a noun job (subject, direct object, indirect object, predicate nominative, or object of the preposition) or if it's being a modifier. It still needs to match the antecedent. That's easy with **definite pronouns** (pronouns that refer to a specific person or thing, like *he*, *she*, *it*, *they*, *I*, *you*, and so on). It's **indefinite pronouns** that might take some thinking about. An **indefinite pronoun** is one that refers to general, nonspecific people or things.

A) **Number** refers to whether a pronoun is singular or plural.

1) The following indefinite pronouns are *singular*; that is, they refer to a single person or thing. They take the singular form of the verb.

each	*one*	*everybody*	*someone*
either	*anybody*	*everyone*	*nobody*
neither	*anyone*	*somebody*	*no one*

Examples: **Each** of the girls **has** her ball and glove. (*There are several girls and they each have their own balls and gloves.*)

One of the boys often **forgets** his coat at school. (*There are several boys, but only one of them forgets his coat.*)

2) The following indefinite pronouns can be either **singular or plural**, depending on the antecedent. Pay careful attention to make sure you use the correct form of the verb.

all	*any*	*some*	*none*

Examples: **Some** of the **students** look funny in **their** costumes. (*There are several students, and more than one of them look funny in their costumes.*)

Some of the **milk** spilled when **it** was poured. (*There was an amount of milk, and a part of it spilled.*)

All of the **cookies** are gone because John ate them! (***Cookies** is plural, so **all** is, too.*)

All of the **pizza** is gone because he ate that, too! (***Pizza** is singular, so **all** is, too.*)

3) Two or more singular antecedents joined by *or* or *nor* are singular.

Examples: Either Bill **or** Ted will bring **his** camera.

Neither Jessica **nor** Julia would repeat what **she** said.

B) **Gender** refers to whether the pronoun is masculine, feminine, or neutral. Is the antecedent a boy noun, a girl noun, or something else? Is it gender neutral, or is the gender unknown?

> **Examples:** The wagon lost one of **its** wheels. (The antecedent is gender neutral; use **it/its**.)
>
> The woman said **her** feet were tired. (The antecedent is feminine; use **she/hers/her**.)
>
> Richard took **his** time. (The antecedent is masculine; use **he/his/him**.)
>
> The postal carrier finished **their** route. (We don't know the antecedent's gender; use **their/theirs**.)

Some older grammar textbooks might say to use **he or she** if the gender of the antecedent is unknown. Some even older ones might say to just use **he** if you don't know the gender! But the rule today is to use **they** if you don't know the gender of the antecedent, and you're talking about a person.

C) **Person** refers to how someone involved in the situation is being talked about.

- Is the person speaking part of the action? This is called **first person**.

First Person Pronouns				
I	me	my	mine	myself
we	us	ourselves	our	ours

- Is the person speaking talking to the person doing the action? This is called **second person**.

Second Person Pronouns		
you	your	yours

- Is the person speaking talking about someone or something else doing the action? This is called **third person**.

Third Person Pronouns				
he	she	it	they	their
him	her	one	them	theirs
his	hers	its		

The **person** of the pronoun must agree (be the same as) the **person** of its antecedent.

Examples:

> Incorrect: **One** should let **your** feelings show. (*One* is third person and *your* is second person.)
>
> Correct: **One** should let **one's** feelings show. (Both pronouns are third person.)
>
> or: **One** should let **their** feelings show. (Both pronouns are third person.)
>
> Incorrect: **I** find that reading in dim light is hard on **your** eyes. (*I* is first person and *your* is second person.
>
> Correct: **I** find that reading in dim light is hard on **my** eyes. (Both pronouns are first person.)

12 EXERCISE A

Pronoun-Antecedent Agreement: Exercise A

Directions
In the sentences below, circle the correct pronoun so that it agrees with its antecedent. Look at the lesson notes for help.

Sentences 1 and 2 focus on pronouns that agree with their antecedents in **number**.

1) Jenna always is very careful to complete (**her**, their) homework every evening.

2) The soldiers were ready for (his, **their**) inspection.

Sentences 3 and 4 focus on pronouns that agree with their antecedents in **gender**.

3) My little brother picked up his train by (**its**, his, her) chimney.

4) Laura put her doll away in (its, **her**, his) box.

Sentences 5 and 6 focus on pronouns that agree with their antecedents in **person**.

5) One should always put away (**one's**, your) toys.

6) If we work together, (you, **we**) can keep our play area neat.

Directions
Edit the following sentences using the editing marks you have learned. If you find a pronoun that disagrees with its antecedent, cross it out and write the correct pronoun above it. There are seven errors. Look back at your notes if you need help.

7) Neither Mikey nor Lucas seems to be able to pick up after ~~themselves~~ *himself*. My mom decided to make them, a list of their daily chores. "I'll check off each chore you do," she said. Mikey's list wasn't very long because he is, younger. Mom says that lucas, on the other hand, needs to be reminded the most often.

Exercise A 12

Directions

In each sentence below there is a comma split. All of the commas in each sentence and the lines below them are numbered. Identify the comma split and write its number in the space next to the sentence number. On the lines under each, write what the comma is splitting on the appropriate line. On the other lines, write the "buzzword" for that punctuation rule. Remember that each pair of quotation marks only counts as one thing. There is a number under either the open quote mark or the entire title, but there is not one under the close quote mark.

___1___ 8) Mom and Dad, try to keep our house at 615 Oak Avenue, Dayton, Ohio, as neat as possible.
                                    1   2   3

    #1   *splits subject and verb*

    #2   *capitalize*

    #3   *names, dates, & places*

___3___ 9) "Lucas," she said, "please read, the chart which lists your chores, Mikey's chores, and mine."
               1   2   3   4

    #1   *quotation marks*

    #2   *gear change comma*

    #3   *splits verb and direct object*

    #4   *items in a series*

___3___ 10) Everybody in our family needs to do their chores every day, and then we will have a neat, home.
                                                                1   2   3

    #1   *pro-ant agr*

    #2   *compound sentence*

    #3   *splits noun and adjective*

12 EXERCISE B

Pronoun-Antecedent Agreement: Exercise B

Directions
In the sentences below, circle the correct pronoun so that it agrees with its antecedent. Look at the lesson notes for help.

Sentences 1 and 2 focus on pronouns that agree with their antecedents in **number**.

1) Each family has (**its**, their) own set of rules about chores.

2) Two of the families in our neighborhood change (its, **their**) list each week.

Sentences 3 and 4 focus on pronouns that agree with their antecedents in **gender**.

3) Sometimes it's Dad who decides what (**he**, she, it) wants.

4) It's easier to do chores when Mom tells (you, **me**) what to do.

Sentences 5 and 6 focus on pronouns that agree with their antecedents in **person**.

5) A person shouldn't just tell other families what (he, **they**) should do.

6) Once you make a plan, however, (**you**, one) should stick to it.

Directions
Edit the following sentences using the editing marks you have learned. If you find a pronoun that disagrees with its antecedent, cross it out and write the correct pronoun above it. There are eight errors. Look back at your notes if you need help.

7) Our neat‸ beautiful house had just been cleaned. We were⟋ ready for a visit from my uncle, Mr. Ray Johnson‸Jr. He is the well-known author of the book <u>A Boy's Guide to Housework</u>. My famous uncle⟋ firmly believes that housework is everyone's responsibility. Nobody in ~~its~~ *our* house will forget their chores when Uncle Ray is here!

EXERCISE B 12

Directions

In each sentence below there is a comma split. All of the commas in each sentence and the lines below them are numbered. Identify the comma split and write its number in the space next to the sentence number. On the lines under each, write what the comma is splitting on the appropriate line. On the other lines, write the "buzzword" for that punctuation rule. Remember that each pair of quotation marks only counts as one thing. There is a number under the open quote mark or the entire title, but there is not one under the close quote mark.

__3__ 8) Uncle Ray thoroughly approves of my mom's clever, chart.
                           1   2   3

   #1 *capitalize*

   #2 *possessives*

   #3 *splits noun and adjective*

__2__ 9) As a matter of fact, he has, a chapter in his book called "The Magic of Charts."
                    1   2   3

   #1 *expressions (or introductory element)*

   #2 *splits verb and direct object*

   #3 *titles*

__2__ 10) Sometimes one of us forgets their chores for the day, but Uncle Ray is, a believer in making
                                                              1   2

   each morning a fresh, new start.
                        3

   #1 *compound sentence*

   #2 *splits linking verb and complement*

   #3 *two adjectives tests*

INSTRUCTOR HANDBOOK — ANALYTICAL GRAMMAR: LEVEL 2 - MECHANICS • LESSON 12 • EXERCISE B

12 EXERCISE C

Pronoun-Antecedent Agreement: Exercise C

Directions
In the sentences below, circle the correct pronoun so that it agrees with its antecedent in **number**, **gender**, and **person**.

1) Both of my brothers have (his, (**their**)) rooms to clean.

2) Only one of them is able to make (their, (**his**)) own bed.

3) "Mikey, you should always make ((**your**), his) bed," I tell him.

4) He tries his best, but his comforter always slips out of ((**its**), his) place.

5) Neither Mikey nor Lucas is really good at making ((**his**), their) bed.

6) I believe that making my bed is one of ((**my**), your) most important chores.

Directions
Edit the following sentences using the editing marks you have learned. If you find a pronoun that disagrees with its antecedent, cross it out and write the correct pronoun above it. There are seven errors. Look back at your notes if you need help.

7) In Uncle ray's book, he teaches boys a song to sing to help ~~him~~ *them* learn to make their beds. This great little song, is called "Sheets and Pillows, Spread 'Em Up!" Putting something to music, after all, helps you remember what to do more easily. Mikey may not be able to make his bed perfectly, but he sure can sing, that song!

EXERCISE C **12**

Directions

In each sentence below there is a comma split. All of the commas in each sentence and the lines below them are numbered. Identify the comma split and write its number in the space next to the sentence number. On the lines under each, write what the comma is splitting on the appropriate line. On the other lines, write the "buzzword" for that punctuation rule. Remember that each pair of quotation marks only counts as one thing. There is a number under the open quote mark or the entire title, but there is not one under the close quote mark.

__3__ 8) "Have you ever noticed," asked Mom, "how easy it is to remember things when they are in
               1   2

a lively, tune?"
       3

    #1   *quotation marks*

    #2   *gear change comma*

    #3   *splits noun and adjective*

__2__ 9) "Sheets and Pillows, Spread 'Em Up" is, a great little song, and it'll result in a neat,
            1   2   3   4

beautiful bed.

    #1   *titles*

    #2   *splits linking verb and complement*

    #3   *compound sentence*

    #4   *two adjectives tests*

__2__ 10) Yes, my Uncle Ray, is a firm believer in learning to make one's bed properly.
              1   2   3

    #1   *introductory element*

    #2   *splits subject and verb*

    #3   *possessives*

12 ASSESSMENT

Pronoun-Antecedent Agreement: Assessment

Directions
In the sentences below, circle the correct pronoun so that it agrees with its antecedent in **number**, **gender**, and **person**.

Each correctly chosen word is worth one point.

__1__ 1) My mom has two brothers, and each of them is an expert in ((his,) their) field.
  1

__1__ 2) Each of my Uncle Bill's books has ((its,) their) own subject.
  1

__1__ 3) If anybody wants to know something, (he, (they)) usually ask Uncle Bill.
  1

__1__ 4) One of his books is on engine repair, and each type of engine has (his, (its))
  1   own chapter.

__1__ 5) I believe that each driver should learn to keep (his, (their)) engine in good condition.
  1

__1__ 6) Each of my uncles has certainly made ((his,) their) parents proud!
  1

  6

Directions
Edit the following sentences using the editing marks you have learned. There are six errors.

Each corrected error is worth one point.

7) My favorite of Uncle Bill's books is called Training Service Dogs. This fantastic book, teaches people how to train dogs for people who are visually impaired, have a disability, or are seniors. There is, after all, a great need for these wonderful dogs. One of his readers has trained a french poodle that is now a service dog for a man with a disability. Everyone who needs a little extra help, should have a great companion like Rocket!

  6

Assessment 12

Directions

In each sentence below there is a comma split. All of the commas in each sentence and the lines below them are numbered. Identify the comma split and write its number in the space next to the sentence number. On the lines under each, write what the comma is splitting on the appropriate line. On the other lines, write the "buzzword" for that punctuation rule. Remember that each pair of quotation marks only counts as one thing. There is a number under the open quote mark or the entire title, but there is not one under the close quote mark.

Identifying the comma split is worth two points. Identifying what is split and which buzzwords apply is worth one point each.

$\frac{2}{2}$ **8)** "Service dogs have, an important job," says my Uncle Bill.
                1   2   3

    $\frac{}{1}$ #1 *quotation marks*

    $\frac{}{1}$ #2 *splits verb and direct object*

    $\frac{}{1}$ #3 *gear change comma*

$\frac{3}{2}$ **9)** Each dog does its job to help its human, and each dog becomes, a great companion.
                                1   2   3

    $\frac{}{1}$ #1 *pro-ant agr*

    $\frac{}{1}$ #2 *compound sentence*

    $\frac{}{1}$ #3 *splits linking verb and complement*

$\frac{3}{2}$ **10)** As a matter of fact, I, would love to learn to train these wonderful, magnificent dogs
                                1 2   3

when I grow up.

    $\frac{}{1}$ #1 *introductory element (or expressions)*

    $\frac{}{1}$ #2 *splits subject and verb*

    $\frac{}{1}$ #3 *two adjectives tests*

$\frac{}{15}$

$\frac{}{27}$ Total Points $\frac{22}{27} = 80\%$

Lesson 13
Subject-Verb Agreement

Lesson 13: Subject-Verb Agreement

The buzzword for this rule is *subj-verb agr.*

Now that we've learned about pronoun-antecedent agreement, there's another kind of grammar agreement you need to know. In the sentences we write, the subject and the verb need to **agree**. In other words, a **singular subject** takes a **singular verb**. A **plural subject** takes a **plural verb**. If you are a native English speaker, you probably do this without even thinking about it!

Examples: One girl jumps.

singular subject: girl (*only one girl*)

singular verb: jumps (*The singular form of the verb usually has an -s added to the end of the word.*)

Three girls jump.

plural subject: girls (*three girls, not just one*)

plural verb: jump (*The plural form of the verb does not have an added -s.*)

Note: It might help to think of it like this: If the subject has an added *-s* (because it's plural), the verb **does not** end in *-s*. Pretend there's only one *-s* to share between the subject and the verb. If the subject needs it to be plural, the verb can't have it. If the subject is singular, then the verb uses it!

Again, you probably already do this without thinking about it much. But there are a few situations where we need to pay attention to do it correctly.

A) When there are modifiers (especially prepositional phrases) between the subject and the verb:

Examples: A **group** (of children) **was** waving to the band.

In this tricky sentence, you can determine the real subject by taking out any modifiers and looking at what's left. **Group** is a singular noun—just one group, even though it may be made up of many children. If we strip out the modifier—the prepositional phrase *of children*—we have **A group was waving to the band**. You wouldn't say *A group* **were** *waving*, because that sounds funny.

A flock of seagulls runs so far away.

Again, determine the real subject by taking out any modifiers. It's easy to see that the verb should be **runs** when we know that the subject is **flock** and not **seagulls**. **Seagulls** is part of a prepositional phrase that tells us what kind of **flock**.

B) When the subject is an **indefinite pronoun:** Look back at the notes for the last lesson to see a list of them again. You learned which of them are singular and which are plural—and which could be either one, depending on the antecedent! Just figure out what the pronoun is replacing (the antecedent) and you'll know whether to use a singular or plural verb.

Examples: Each of the boys **is** a good singer. (**Each** *takes a singular verb because it is talking about the individual boys. "That boy is a good singer, and so is that boy."*)

Both of the boys **are** good singers. (**Both** *takes a plural verb because it is talking about two boys together: "The two boys are good singers."*)

Take out the modifiers and strip the sentences down, then read just the subject and the verb: **Each is** and **Both are**. If you said **Each are** or **Both is**, it sounds funny because they don't agree in number.

Here's where it's a little tricky. Remember this example?

All of the cookies **are** gone because John ate them! (**All** *is plural in this sentence, because its antecedent is* **cookies**. *It takes the plural verb* **are**.)

All of the pizza **is** gone because John ate it! (**All** *is singular in this sentence, because its antecedent is a single* **pizza**. *It takes the singular verb* **is**.)

For some indefinite pronouns, you will need to make sure you know what the antecedent is, because that is how you will know whether you need a singular verb or a plural verb.

C) When singular subjects are joined by a **conjunction**: The conjunction **and** joins things together, so, just like in math, one plus one is two. And two is plural!

John **is** tall. (*singular subject, singular verb*)

Martha **is** tall. (*singular subject, singular verb*)

John **and** Martha **are** tall. (**and** *makes a plural subject, so now you need a plural verb*)

Other conjunctions, like **either/or** and **neither/nor** (or **nor** or **or** alone), do not combine things into a plural. Quite the opposite: they keep singular subjects singular. So you need to use a singular verb with them.

John **or** Martha **is** helping with the decorations.

John **and** Martha **are** helping with the decorations.

Neither the teacher **nor** the student **was** on time.

Both the teacher **and** the student **were** late.

13 EXERCISE A

Subject-Verb Agreement: Exercise A

Directions
In the sentences below, circle the correct verb that agrees with the subject.

1) Each of the families in my taekwondo class (**is,** are) planning what they want to do for Thanksgiving.

2) Two of them (is, **are**) traveling to visit their grandparents.

3) Neither of those two families (**is,** are) traveling very far, though.

4) Last year most of the kids (was, **were**) just staying at home.

5) But this year nobody in any of the classes (**is,** are) staying at home.

Directions
Mark the errors in the following sentences. Look out for subject-verb agreement. If you need to change a verb, draw a line through the incorrect one and write the correct verb above it.

Example: ~~are~~ *is*

There are seven errors.

6) Neither my mom nor my dad ~~were~~ *was* very excited about staying home last year. "To be honest," said my mom, "it's just a lot of work for our whole family!" She said she'd be more than, happy to let someone else do the cooking this year! As a matter of fact, I really enjoy playing with my cousins' toys at their house. Of course, we always take, a special side dish to help out with dinner. I just love the turkey, stuffing, mashed potatoes, and cranberry sauce. I can almost smell the delicious, tempting aroma of pumpkin pie right now!

128 ANALYTICAL GRAMMAR: LEVEL 2 - MECHANICS • LESSON 13 • EXERCISE A   INSTRUCTOR HANDBOOK

Directions

In each sentence below there is a comma split. All of the commas in each sentence and the lines below them are numbered. Identify the comma split and write its number in the space next to the sentence number. On the lines under each, write what the comma is splitting on the appropriate line. On the other lines, write the "buzzword" for that punctuation rule. Remember that each pair of quotation marks only counts as one thing. There is a number under the open quote mark or the entire title, but there is not one under the close quote mark.

__3__ 7) At the beginning of Thanksgiving dinner, all of us, take turns saying what we're thankful for.
                                  1   2   3

    #1   *capitalize*

    #2   *introductory element*

    #3   *splits subject and verb*

__4__ 8) "I'm thankful for my family, my friends, and my dog Coco," said my little, cousin Samantha.
          1   2   3   4

    #1   *quotation marks*

    #2   *item in a series*

    #3   *gear change comma*

    #4   *splits noun and adjective*

__1__ 9) It is also, a custom for our family to sing "Bless This House," and we've gotten pretty good at it!
                     1   2   3

    #1   *splits linking verb and complement*

    #2   *titles*

    #3   *compound sentence (or gear change comma)*

13 EXERCISE B

Subject-Verb Agreement: Exercise B

Directions
In the sentences below, circle the correct verb that agrees with the subject.

1) Unfortunately, neither my dad nor my brother ((sings,) sing) very well.

2) Each of the other family members ((tries,) try) to sing really loudly to drown them out.

3) After the song, everybody in our family ((pitches,) pitch) in to clean up.

4) Neither my little niece nor my baby brother ((is,) are) to be trusted with clearing the table.

5) One of my older family members ((is,) are) always in charge of handling the china.

Directions
Mark the errors in the following sentences using the editing marks you have learned. There are seven errors. (**Hint:** Remember that quotation marks count as just one error!)

6) This year, Thanksgiving was on Thursday, November 26, which was also my dad's birthday! Everybody else in the family, decided to make an extra big pumpkin pie with candles on it. Then, after we sang our Thanksgiving song, we all sang the song "Happy Birthday." As a matter of fact, Dad was pretty pleased with our surprise birthday pie. He gave my mom, a big hug and said, "Thanks, Honey!"

EXERCISE B **13**

Directions
In each sentence below there is a comma split. All of the commas in each sentence and the lines below them are numbered. Identify the comma split and write its number in the space next to the sentence number. On the lines under each, write what the comma is splitting on the appropriate line. On the other lines, write the "buzzword" for that punctuation rule. Remember that each pair of quotation marks only counts as one thing. There is a number under the open quote mark or the entire title, but there is not one under the close quote mark.

__2__ 7) Yes, we have several Thanksgiving, traditions in our family, but my favorite one involves
           1   2   3

my uncles.

   #1 _introductory element_

   #2 _splits noun and adjective_

   #3 _compound sentence_

__1__ 8) Each uncle sits everyone down and tells us, an outrageous, elaborate story about his
                                                 1   2   3

younger days.

   #1 _splits indirect object and direct object_

   #2 _two adjectives tests_

   #3 _pro-ant agr_

__2__ 9) Uncle Joe's stories are usually, completely untrue, as a matter of fact!
                      1   2   3

   #1 _possessives_

   #2 _splits linking verb and complement_

   #3 _expressions_

13 EXERCISE C

Subject-Verb Agreement: Exercise C

Directions
In the sentences below, circle the correct verb that agrees with the subject.

1) All of my uncles (tries, (try)) to outdo each other with their stories.

2) Neither Uncle Bill nor Uncle Jay ((is), are) able to top Uncle Joe's stories.

3) Each of them (try, (tries)) really hard every year, but usually Uncle Joe wins.

4) A small group of us children ((votes), vote) on whose story is the best.

5) This year nobody ((was), were) hesitant; the winner was Uncle Joe again!

Directions
Mark the errors in the following sentences using the editing marks you have learned. There are six errors. (Hint: Remember that quotation marks count as just one error!)

6) This year, Uncle Joe's story was called "The Night They Burned the Outhouse." He swears this story took place on October 31, 1995, in the town where he grew up. The story, involves his best friend, his high school football coach, and an old outhouse. No one in our family actually believes Uncle Joe, but we sure have a great time listening to him!

EXERCISE C **13**

Directions
In each sentence below there is a comma split. All of the commas in each sentence and the lines below them are numbered. Identify the comma split and write its number in the space next to the sentence number. On the lines under each, write what the comma is splitting on the appropriate line. On the other lines, write the "buzzword" for that punctuation rule. Remember that each pair of quotation marks only counts as one thing. There is a number under the open quote mark or the entire title, but there is not one under the close quote mark.

_2_ 7) Uncle Jay's story this year was called, "Mrs. Sherwood's Old Grey Sweater."
          1   2 3

   #1 _possessives_

   #2 _splits verb and direct object_

   #3 _titles_

_3_ 8) Yes, it's about one of his teachers from Elmwood Elementary who had, this ratty old
        1   2   3
   gray sweater.

   #1 _introductory element_

   #2 _capitalize_

   #3 _splits verb and direct object_

_3_ 9) The sweater went missing one day, but he claims that neither he nor his friend
                                        1
   was, responsible!
    2 3

   #1 _compound sentence_

   #2 _sub-verb agr_

   #3 _splits linking verb and complement_

INSTRUCTOR HANDBOOK   ANALYTICAL GRAMMAR: LEVEL 2 - MECHANICS • LESSON 13 • EXERCISE C

13 ASSESSMENT

Subject-Verb Agreement: Assessment

Directions
In the sentences below, circle the correct verb that agrees with the subject.

Each correctly chosen word is worth one point.

___1) Both Uncle Jay and Uncle Joe (**(remember,)** remembers) Uncle Bill's story.
  1

___2) Once an old pair of Uncle Bill's jeans (**(was,)** were) eaten by a goat!
  1

___3) Each of my uncles (insist, **(insists)**) that this is a true story.
  1

___4) Either Uncle Jay or Uncle Joe (**(was,)** were) also there when the goat ate the pants.
  1

___5) It happened when a herd of goats (**(was,)** were) quietly grazing in a meadow.
  1

  ==
  5

Directions
Mark the errors in the following sentences using the editing marks you have learned. There are seven errors. (Hint: Remember that quotation marks count as just one error!)

Each corrected error is worth one point.

6) According to Uncle Bill's story, he and one of his brothers set out for a walk on a hot, steamy summer day. Uncle Bill was wearing his favorite pair of jeans that had not been washed for weeks! He got so hot that he decided to jump in the creek and hung his jeans on the meadow fence. One curious goat came over and started to sniff Uncle Bill's jeans. The dirty, sweaty jeans must have smelled interesting to the goat, because she started to eat them! "Let go of my jeans!" yelled Uncle Bill. This is how we learned the story "The Day the Goat Ate My Jeans" by uncle Bill.

  ==
  7

134 ANALYTICAL GRAMMAR: LEVEL 2 - MECHANICS • LESSON 13 • ASSESSMENT   INSTRUCTOR HANDBOOK

Assessment 13

Directions

In each sentence below there is a comma split. All of the commas in each sentence and the lines below them are numbered. Identify the comma split and write its number in the space next to the sentence number. On the lines under each, write what the comma is splitting on the appropriate line. On the other lines, write the "buzzword" for that punctuation rule. Remember that each pair of quotation marks only counts as one thing. There is a number under the open quote mark or the entire title, but there is not one under the close quote mark.

Identifying the comma split is worth two points. Identifying what is split and which buzzwords apply is worth one point each.

__2__ / _2_   7) Needless to say, the whole family loves to hear my uncles' stories after Thanksgiving,
                                                                                              1   2

dinner, but each year they have to work harder to outdo each other.
      3

    __ / _1_ #1 *expressions (or introductory element)*
    __ / _1_ #2 *splits noun and adjective*
    __ / _1_ #3 *compound sentence*

__4__ / _2_   8) After the vote from all the kids, we declared Uncle Joe the winner of this year's
                                                                        1   2   3

story-telling, contest.
          4

    __ / _1_ #1 *introductory element*
    __ / _1_ #2 *capitalize*
    __ / _1_ #3 *possessives*
    __ / _1_ #4 *splits noun and adjective*

__3__ / _2_   9) "Just wait until next year," exclaimed Uncle Jay, "and I'll beat, you yet!"
          1   2   3

    __ / _1_ #1 *quotation marks*
    __ / _1_ #2 *gear change comma*
    __ / _1_ #3 *splits verb and direct object*

__ / _16_

__ / _28_ *Total Points* $\dfrac{22}{28} = 80\%$

Lesson 14
Which Pronoun?

Lesson 14: Which Pronoun?

The buzzword for this lesson is **which pronoun**.

There are four groups of pronouns: personal, demonstrative, interrogative, and indefinite. Today's lesson will explain in which situations to use certain personal pronouns. Let's take a look at this list of personal pronouns:

Personal pronouns

Nominative Case	Objective Case
I	me
you	you
he	him
she	her
it	it
we	us
they	them
who*	whom*
whoever*	whomever*

*These aren't personal pronouns; they're interrogatives, or pronouns that ask questions and don't have to have an antecedent. But the answers to the questions they can ask will be people (think: persons!), so they are included on these lists.

Did you notice the labels on the tops of the columns? **Nominative** and **objective** are just fancy names that tell you where you need to use these pronouns.

Examples: I went to the store.

Maria went with I to the store.

Hmmm. The first one is fine, but the second one doesn't sound right. Why not? After all, the speaker is talking about themself in both sentences. *I* and *me* both talk about the same person. But if you were to diagram the sentences, you would see that *I* is the subject in the first sentence and the object of the preposition in the second.

Examples: Me went to the store.

Maria went with me to the store.

Now the second sentence sounds fine, but the first one is wrong! *Me* sounds silly as a subject, although it's fine as the object of the preposition. That's because *I* is in the **nominative case**, while *me* in the **objective case**. Here's the difference:

Nominative case is used for subjects and predicate nominatives. *Nominative* is even part of the name.

Objective case is used for direct objects, indirect objects, and objects of the preposition. You can see the word *object* in the name!

So why do you need to know all this stuff? Well, if you use the wrong case, your sentence could sound like baby talk (*Me went to the store*) or like you might be trying too hard to sound smart (*Maria went with I to the store*).

If you're a native English speaker, you can probably tell which one "sounds right" most of the time. But knowing for sure can be tricky, especially with compound subjects or objects. Almost all of us use incorrect grammar when we're not thinking hard about it for school and we're just talking to our friends and families. And that's okay! But sometimes we want to be extra sure that we're correct. If you're not sure whether you need to use the nominative or objective case in a compound subject or object, try this: **take the other person out**. Sometimes you can tell just by listening to which one sounds right. If you can't tell from listening, that's when your knowledge of grammar will help you.

Examples: Which is correct?

> Give the package to Bob or I. **or** Give the package to Bob or me.

Let's take Bob out of it. Now, which sounds correct?

> Give the package to I. **or** Give the package to me.

Me sounds right, so the whole sentence should be *Give the package to Bob or me*. If you're still not sure, use your grammar skills to check. With Bob out of the way, it's easier to see that *me* is the object of the prepositional phrase *to me* and that you need to use the objective case **me**.

How about this one:

> She and Tommy had a great time. **or** Her and Tommy had a great time.

If we take Tommy out of it, we have:

> She had a great time. **or** Her had a great time.

She sounds right, doesn't it? And we know, using grammar, that it's because *she* is the subject of the sentence. Subject pronouns need to be in the nominative case. If we add Tommy back in, the correct sentence should read *She and Tommy had a great time*.

There are a couple more guidelines for compound subjects or objects that are based on etiquette, or the rules about being polite.

- When you use the personal pronouns *I* or *me* along with another noun, always **put the other guy first**. Imagine that you need to squeeze through a narrow hallway, but there is another person coming from the other direction. The polite thing to do is to stand aside and let them go first. The same thing is true about grammar!

    Example: incorrect: He told **me and Jeff** to come back later.

    correct: He told **Jeff and me** to come back later.

- What if you have a whole list of people? You know that you should put yourself last in most cases, but how do the other people get ordered? Imagine that you are going to a restaurant with your whole extended family: your parents, aunts and uncles, and grandparents. You get to the door first, because you're young and fast! But you're also polite, so you hold the door open for the adults. Your grandparents go first, because they're the eldest. Then your aunts and uncles probably go next, since they are guests. Finally, your immediate family: your parents go next, and then you. It's the same with people and pronouns. The polite order is **oldest to youngest** and **farthest to closest**. Here's an example:

    Example: incorrect: My dad, my aunt, my grandpa and I went to the sprint car races.

    correct: My grandpa, my aunt, my dad, and I went to the sprint car races.

14 EXERCISE A

Which Pronoun?: Exercise A

Directions
In the sentences below, circle the correct word or group of words. Look back at the notes if you need help.

1) (Me and my brother / **My brother and I**) decided to have a reading contest.

2) (Him and me / **He and I**) love to read adventure and mystery stories.

3) Every week (**my mom, my brother, and I** / my brother, my mom, and I) go to the library.

4) We always ask the librarian to save the good new books for (Jason and I / **Jason and me**).

5) Mom always challenges (**Jason and me** / Jason and I) to see who can read the most pages every day.

Directions
Mark the errors in the following sentences using the editing marks you have learned. There are seven errors. If you need to change a pronoun to another case, cross it out and write the correct word above.

6) My brother and ~~me~~ *I* have recently discovered the Hardy Boys series of books. Yes, these are old books, but they're really fun to read. My cousins, love the Nancy Drew series, which became popular about the same time as the Hardy Boys. In the Nancy drew books, Nancy, Bess, and George are best friends who solve all kinds of mysteries. In the case of the Hardy Boys, the two Hardy brothers, Frank and Joe, also stumble upon all kinds of mysteries and solve them.

EXERCISE A **14**

Directions
In each sentence below there is a comma split. All of the commas in each sentence and the lines below them are numbered. Identify the comma split and write its number in the space next to the sentence number. On the lines under each, write what the comma is splitting on the appropriate line. On the other lines, write the "buzzword" for that punctuation rule. Remember that each pair of quotation marks only counts as one thing. There is a number under the open quote mark or the entire title, but there is not one under the close quote mark.

_2_ 7) When my brother and I, go to the library, there are so many Hardy Boys books to choose from!
               12   3

   #1 *which pronoun?*

   #2 *splits subject and verb*

   #3 *capitalize*

_3_ 8) As a matter of fact, Hardy Boys books have been written since 1927, and they are still, popular.
                    1   2   3

   #1 *introductory element (or expressions)*

   #2 *compound sentence*

   #3 *splits linking verb and complement*

_2_ 9) These exciting, adventurous stories are now called, *Hardy Boys: Undercover Brothers*.
                   1   2   3

   #1 *two adjectives tests*

   #2 *splits verb and direct object*

   #3 *titles*

INSTRUCTOR HANDBOOK   ANALYTICAL GRAMMAR: LEVEL 2 - MECHANICS • LESSON 14 • EXERCISE A **141**

14 EXERCISE B

Which Pronoun?: Exercise B

Directions
In the sentences below, circle the correct word or group of words. Look back at the notes if you need help.

1) Finally my mom said that (my brother and me / (my brother and I)) had to stop reading Hardy Boys mysteries and try something different.

2) The librarian knows what we like, so she saves all the good new books for ((Jason and me) / me and Jason).

3) Reagan and Molly, our cousins, use the same library, and ((she and Molly) / her and Molly) think we have the best librarian in the world!

4) (Reagan, Molly, and Aunt Ruth / (Aunt Ruth, Reagan, and Molly)) try to visit the library once a week at the same time we go.

5) After we get our new books, (their family and us / (their family and we)) all go to lunch together.

Directions
Mark the errors in the following sentences using the editing marks you have learned. There are seven errors.

6) Aunt Ruth says her first Nancy drew book was, The Secret in the Old Clock. She got it from her Uncle Bill for her birthday on April 18, 2001. She says she didn't think it would be that interesting, but she couldn't put it down once she started. "To tell you the truth," she said, "I ended up reading it under the covers with my dad's flashlight!"

EXERCISE B 14

Directions

In each sentence below there is a comma split. All of the commas in each sentence and the lines below them are numbered. Identify the comma split and write its number in the space next to the sentence number. On the lines under each, write what the comma is splitting on the appropriate line. On the other lines, write the "buzzword" for that punctuation rule. Remember that each pair of quotation marks only counts as one thing. There is a number under the open quote mark or the entire title, but there is not one under the close quote mark.

_1_ 7) Aunt Ruth, tells of a time when she had the flu, and her Uncle Bill brought her four new
              1   2   3

Nancy Drew books!

#1 _splits subject and verb_

#2 _compound sentence_

#3 _capitalize_

_3_ 8) Each of her uncles got her what he thought she'd like, but Uncle Bill's gift was, her
                                          1   2   3

very favorite.

#1 _pro-ant agr_

#2 _possessives_

#3 _splits linking verb and complement_

_3_ 9) While she was getting her strength back, Aunt Ruth relaxed and read her wonderful,
                                    1   2

exciting, books.
     3

#1 _capitalize_

#2 _two adjectives tests_

#3 _splits noun and adjective_

14 EXERCISE C

Which Pronoun?: Exercise C

Directions
In the sentences below, circle the correct word or group of words. Look back at the notes if you need help.

1) (**My brother and I** / Me and my brother) also love to read books about true adventures.

2) (**He and I** / Him and me) just finished one about a man who trekked through the jungles of the Amazon.

3) (Him / **He**) and his hiking partners met different people who live in the Amazonian jungle.

4) (**They** / Them) and the indigenous peoples were very curious about each other.

5) He kept a journal for (**him** / he) and his family to read after he got home.

Directions
Mark the errors in the following sentences using the editing marks you have learned. There are eight errors. Be careful—this is a tricky one!

6) ~~Me~~ *I* and jason decided that we are going to go on an adventure when we grow up. To tell you the truth, we haven't decided where we'll go yet, but we sure plan to do it. Then we'll write a book called Two Brothers' Adventures and become famous! Jason's first choice is to climb Mount Everest, but neither of us ~~are~~ *is* sure where we'll really go.

Exercise C 14

Directions

In each sentence below there is a comma split. All of the commas in each sentence and the lines below them are numbered. Identify the comma split and write its number in the space next to the sentence number. On the lines under each, write what the comma is splitting on the appropriate line. On the other lines, write the "buzzword" for that punctuation rule. Remember that each pair of quotation marks only counts as one thing. There is a number under the open quote mark or the entire title, but there is not one under the close quote mark.

__1__ 7) My cousins, also have plans to do something totally, absolutely wonderful, but they haven't
       1   2   3

decided what yet.

 #1 _splits subject and verb_

 #2 _two adjectives tests_

 #3 _compound sentence_

__2__ 8) Well, they can't decide if they want to be, teachers, lawyers, or doctors.
     1   2   3

 #1 _introductory element_

 #2 _splits linking verb and complement_

 #3 _items in a series_

__3__ 9) Reagan's first choice is medicine, and she's already written her doctor, a letter asking for advice.
      1   2   3

 #1 _possessives_

 #2 _compound sentence_

 #3 _splits indirect object and direct object_

14 ASSESSMENT

Which Pronoun?: Assessment

Directions

In the sentences below, circle the correct word or group of words. Look back at the notes if you need help.

Each correctly chosen word or group of words is worth one point.

___ 1) (**(Reagan, Molly, Jason, and I)** / Reagan, me, Molly, and Jason) love to read all
 1   kinds of books.

___ 2) (Us / **(We)**) and our parents are well known at the local library.
 1

___ 3) Every book we read teaches (**(us)** / we) and our cousins something new.
 1

___ 4) Our teacher told (Jason and I / **(Jason and me)**) that reading would increase
 1   our vocabularies.

___ 5) (Me and Jason / **(Jason and I)**) should have the biggest vocabularies in town with
 1   all the reading we do!

=====
 5

Directions

Mark the errors in the following sentences using the editing marks you have learned.
There are seven errors.

Each corrected error is worth one point.

6) Everybody, in my bunch of friends love to read. The best conversation starter at our

    lunch table is, "Guess what I'm reading! After the description of the book we all

    usually want to read the same book. Our latest craze has been The Chronicles of

    Narnia. Our teacher, Miss mitchell, thinks it's pretty funny when we complain about

    book reports. "Guys you give a book report at lunch every day!" she said.

=====
 7

ASSESSMENT 14

Directions

In each sentence below there is a comma split. All of the commas in each sentence and the lines below them are numbered. Identify the comma split and write its number in the space next to the sentence number. On the lines under each, write what the comma is splitting on the appropriate line. On the other lines, write the "buzzword" for that punctuation rule. Remember that each pair of quotation marks only counts as one thing. There is a number under the open quote mark or the entire title, but there is not one under the close quote mark.

Identifying the comma split is worth two points. Identifying what is split and which buzzwords apply is worth one point each.

__3__ 7) Miss Mitchell asked us one day, "What's going on in your head when you're reading,
 2   1   2   3

  a really good book?"

  __ #1 *capitalize*
  1

  __ #2 *gear change comma*
  1

  __ #3 *splits verb and direct object*
  1

__3__ 8) To be honest, we just stared at her at first, but then Michael, slowly raised his hand.
 2   1   2   3

  __ #1 *expressions*
  1

  __ #2 *compound sentence*
  1

  __ #3 *splits subject and verb*
  1

__2__ 9) "Miss Mitchell, last night when I was reading, *The Silver Chair,* I had a whole movie
 2   1   2   3

  going in my head!" he said.

  __ #1 *direct address*
  1

  __ #2 *splits verb and direct object*
  1

  __ #3 *titles*
  1

══
15

══ Total Points $\dfrac{22}{27} = 80\%$
27

Lesson 15
Adjective or Adverb?

Lesson 15: Adjective or Adverb?

The buzzword for this skill is **adj or adv**.

An **adjective** modifies (or describes) a **noun or pronoun**.

*She found the **perfect jacket**!* (*perfect* describes the *jacket*)

An **adverb** modifies (or describes) a **verb**.

*The jacket **fits** her **perfectly**!* (*perfectly* describes how the jacket *fits*)

Sometimes people use an adjective when they should use an adverb.

That jacket fits her perfect!

Unfortunately, **perfect** is an adjective, but in this sentence, it is trying to describe how the jacket **fits**. This is a very common grammatical error. As with many grammar rules, your reader or listener will probably still understand what you mean, so it might not matter in some situations. However, in a case where it is very important that you use proper grammar, this is a good thing to understand.

Two very commonly confused pairs are the adjectives **good** and **bad** versus the adverbs **well** and **badly**.

- *Good* and *bad* are **adjectives** that either modify nouns or pronouns, or act as predicate adjectives.

    Example: It was a **good day**. The **traffic** wasn't **bad**.

- *Well* and *badly* are **adverbs** that modify verbs, adjectives, or other adverbs.

    Example: He **did well** on the test, although he **did badly** on the multiple choice.

> **Note:** The only time **well** should be used as an adjective is when you are describing someone's health.
>
> "How are you feeling?"
>
> "I feel **well**," not "I feel **good**."
>
> However, if you are sick, don't say "I feel **bad**," or even, "I feel **badly**." If you wake up with a sore throat, say, "I ***don't feel well***."

Another way to use modifiers that can cause confusion is when you're comparing two or more things or actions to show which has the **most** or **least** of something. There are special names and forms we use for these comparisons:

The **comparative** form is used to *compare* two words. The **superlative** form is used to compare more than two and to show which has the *most* (or *least*) of what is being compared.

For most **adjectives**, the **comparative** is formed by adding **-er**, and the **superlative** is formed by adding **-est**.

Example: Imagine listening to the engines of three cars: one red, one blue, and one black. How could you describe **how quiet** the cars are, compared to one another?

quiet	The red car is **quiet**.
quieter (*"more quiet" than another thing*)	The blue car is **quieter**. (*than the red car*)
quietest (*the "most quiet" out of all the things*)	The black car is the **quietest**. (*out of all three cars*)

For **adverbs**, add *more* (or *less*) for the **comparative** and *most* (or *least*) for the **superlative**.

Example: Now imagine that you are describing how the cars' engines run. How could you describe *how quietly* they run?

quietly	The red car's engine runs *quietly*.
more quietly	The blue car's engine runs *more quietly* (than the red car's engine runs).
most quietly	The black car's engine runs *most quietly* of all.

15 EXERCISE A

Adjective or Adverb: Exercise A

Directions
Circle the correct word in the sentences below.

1) Jason's mom decided that his school clothes didn't fit (good, **well**) any more.

2) Just six months ago they had fit (perfect, **perfectly**)!

3) Jason just didn't feel (**good,** well) about wearing those short pants to school.

4) He felt (**bad,** badly) that his parents had to spend more money on him so soon.

   (**Hint:** *remember that* felt *is a linking verb!*)

5) His dad said he was just growing so (quick, **quickly**) that there was no help for it!

Directions
Mark the errors in the following sentences using the editing marks you have learned. There are seven errors. If you need to change one word to another to correct any errors, cross it out and write the correct word above.

6) "We need to buy you some new school pants," said Mom. "you'll also need a couple of new shirts." The sweater Jason had been wearing to school still fit ~~good~~ *well*. Jason's mom decided that the next day would be a good day to go shopping, but then she remembered that Jason had a dentist appointment. To tell you the truth, Jason would rather have gone shopping than go to the dentist. He really wasn't afraid of kind, gentle Dr. Mason, but he didn't like the taste of the fluoride treatment!

Directions

In each sentence below there is a comma split. All of the commas in each sentence and the lines below them are numbered. Identify the comma split and write its number in the space next to the sentence number. On the lines under each, write what the comma is splitting on the appropriate line. On the other lines, write the "buzzword" for that punctuation rule. Remember that each pair of quotation marks only counts as one thing. There is a number under the open quote mark or the entire title, but there is not one under the close quote mark.

__2__ 7) At the dentist's office, Jason read his book while he waited for his, appointment with
                             1   2

    Dr. Mason.
        3

    #1 _possessives_

    #2 _splits noun and adjective_

    #3 _capitalize_

__4__ 8) "Let's see how things look, Jason," Dr. Mason, said.
      1   2   3   4

    #1 _quotation marks_

    #2 _direct address_

    #3 _gear change comma_

    #4 _splits linking verb and complement_

__2__ 9) At the end of his appointment, Jason was, proud to announce that his teeth looked perfect.
                              1   2   3

    #1 _introductory element_

    #2 _splits linking verb and complement_

    #3 _adj or adv_

15 EXERCISE B

Adjective or Adverb: Exercise B

Directions
Circle the correct word(s) in the sentences below. Look back at the lesson notes if you need help.

1) The next morning Jason said, "Mom, I don't feel very (good, (**well**))."

2) Mom took his temperature and said, "This doesn't look ((**good**), well)."

3) Jason began to cough ((**more often**), oftener) than he usually did.

4) "It would be ((**good**), well) for you to stay at home today," said Mom.

5) So Jason had to wait (patient, (**patiently**)) for his new school clothes for another day.

Directions
Mark the errors in the following sentences using the editing marks you have learned. There are seven errors. If you need to change one word to another to correct any errors, cross it out and write the correct word above.

6) After a few days of rest, Jason felt better, and Mom decided that they could go shopping for his new shirts and pants. Jason always felt he could use a book called Shopping When You Don't Like Shopping, but Mom knew exactly where to go. She headed for the best store in Elmwood, Ohio. "May I help you?" asked the clerk in the store. They showed Jason two different styles of pants, but neither of them ~~were~~ *was* what he wanted. Jason finally, chose a navy pair of pants, a yellow shirt, and a pale blue t-shirt.

Exercise B 15

Directions

In each sentence below there is a comma split. All of the commas in each sentence and the lines below them are numbered. Identify the comma split and write its number in the space next to the sentence number. On the lines under each, write what the comma is splitting on the appropriate line. On the other lines, write the "buzzword" for that punctuation rule. Remember that each pair of quotation marks only counts as one thing. There is a number under the open quote mark or the entire title, but there is not one under the close quote mark.

__1__ 7) Jason really liked, the way his new shirts fit so smoothly, and his pants were very comfortable.
                       1   2   3

    #1 _splits verb and direct object_

    #2 _adj or adv_

    #3 _compound sentence_

__1__ 8) All his new, clothes went perfectly with his older brother's tan sweater.
                      1   2   3

    #1 _splits noun and adjective_

    #2 _adj or adv_

    #3 _possessives_

__3__ 9) "Yes, you can have my old sweater," said his brother. "I'm not wearing, it anymore."
             1 2   3

    #1 _quotation marks_

    #2 _introductory element_

    #3 _splits verb and direct object_

15 EXERCISE C

Adjective or Adverb: Exercise C

Directions
Circle the correct word in the sentences below. Look at the lesson notes if you need help.

1) On the following Monday, Jason thought he looked (**good**, well) in his new clothes.

2) The sun shone (bright, **brightly**) on him as he walked into school.

3) Since he was a bit late, he walked (quicker, **more quickly**) than usual to his classroom.

4) Jason felt (**handsome**, handsomely) in his new clothes.

5) His buddies teased him and he laughed (good-natured, **good-naturedly**).

Directions
Mark the errors in the following sentences using the editing marks you have learned. There are seven errors. If you need to change one word to another to correct any errors, cross it out and write the correct word above.

6) After school, Jason and his friends greeted Principal newell as they left the building. "How are you Jason?" she asked. "I was sick last week, but now I'm ~~good~~ *well*," Jason replied. Jason's friend Erik noticed Jason's new t-shirt and said it looked very sharp. "I have new pants, two new shirts and a new sweater!" Jason said. "Between you and ~~I~~ *me*," Erik said, "I have the same shirt!"

Exercise C 15

Directions
In each sentence below there is a comma split. All of the commas in each sentence and the lines below them are numbered. Identify the comma split and write its number in the space next to the sentence number. On the lines under each, write what the comma is splitting on the appropriate line. On the other lines, write the "buzzword" for that punctuation rule. Remember that each pair of quotation marks only counts as one thing. There is a number under the open quote mark or the entire title, but there is not one under the close quote mark.

__1__ 7) Jason was very, pleased to have his new clothes praised by his friend Erik, but he didn't
                                          1   2

want to look too proud.

#1 _splits linking verb and complement_

#2 _compound sentence_

__3__ 8) "Well, my mom helped me pick them out," he said, "and she has, really good taste."
              1   2   3

#1 _introductory element_

#2 _gear change comma_

#3 _splits verb and direct object_

__3__ 9) Erik grinned, laughed with Jason, and said, "Yeah, my mom picks out most of my clothes, too!"
                        1   2   3

#1 _items in a series_

#2 _introductory element_

#3 _splits noun and adjective_

15 ASSESSMENT

Adjective or Adverb: Assessment

Directions
Circle the correct word in the sentences below. Look at the lesson notes if you need help.

Each correctly chosen word or group of words is worth one point.

___1) Jason walked (slow, (**slowly**)) on the way home from school.
 1

___2) At home, his older brother noticed that Jason was ((**quieter,**) more quietly)
 1   than usual.

___3) "Are you feeling (good, (**well**)), buddy?" asked Jason's brother.
 1

___4) "I am afraid I bragged too (proud, (**proudly**)) about my new clothes,"
 1   Jason admitted.

___5) "That's okay," said his brother. "Most people feel ((**good,**) well) about themselves
 1   when they have new clothes."

___
 5

Directions
Mark the errors in the following sentences using the editing marks you have learned. There are seven errors. If you need to change one word to another to correct any errors, cross it out and write the correct word above.

Each corrected error is worth one point.

6) "I distinctly, remember a time when I was wearing a new pair of shoes," said Mom.

"My mother and ~~me~~ I were in a store, and I spotted a friend of mine from school. My

mother, told me there was no need to mention my new shoes. I gave my mother, a

look, because I didn't understand why I shouldn't mention my shoes. On the other hand,

I didn't want to disobey her. As soon as I saw my friend's eyes look down toward my

shoes, however, I couldn't resist shouting out that they were new!"

___
 7

158 ANALYTICAL GRAMMAR: LEVEL 2 - MECHANICS • LESSON 15 • ASSESSMENT   INSTRUCTOR HANDBOOK

ASSESSMENT 15

Directions

In each sentence below there is a comma split. All of the commas in each sentence and the lines below them are numbered. Identify the comma split and write its number in the space next to the sentence number. On the lines under each, write what the comma is splitting on the appropriate line. On the other lines, write the "buzzword" for that punctuation rule. Remember that each pair of quotation marks only counts as one thing. There is a number under the open quote mark or the entire title, but there is not one under the close quote mark.

Identifying the comma split is worth two points. Identifying what is split and which buzzwords apply is worth one point each.

$\frac{2}{2}$ 7) "Look at my new shoes!" I shouted. "We just bought, them at Leonard's Department Store!"
                1   2   3

$\frac{\ }{1}$ #1 *quotation marks*
$\frac{\ }{1}$ #2 *splits verb and direct object*
$\frac{\ }{1}$ #3 *capitalize*

$\frac{2}{2}$ 8) "Margaret, what did I tell you?" asked my, mother. "Why, you did exactly what I asked
                      1   2   3

you not to do!"

$\frac{\ }{1}$ #1 *direct address*
$\frac{\ }{1}$ #2 *splits noun and adjective*
$\frac{\ }{1}$ #3 *introductory element*

$\frac{1}{2}$ 9) I was immediately, sorry that I had bragged about my new shoes, but I had been
                               1   2

unable to resist the interest on my friend's face.
                                 3

$\frac{\ }{1}$ #1 *splits linking verb and complement*
$\frac{\ }{1}$ #2 *compound sentence*
$\frac{\ }{1}$ #3 *possessives*

$\frac{\ }{15}$

$\frac{\ }{27}$ Total Points $\frac{22}{27} = 80\%$

INSTRUCTOR HANDBOOK   ANALYTICAL GRAMMAR: LEVEL 2 - MECHANICS • LESSON 15 • ASSESSMENT   159

Lesson 16
Transitive and Intransitive Verbs

Lesson 16: Transitive and Intransitive Verbs

The buzzword for this lesson is *transitive/intransitive verbs*.

Before we get into this lesson's topic, stop for a moment and take this in: This is the last lesson in the book; the very last one in the whole book! If you want to do a quick dance or sing a song to celebrate, we'll wait...

Okay, now sit down and let's finish this thing!

Action verbs express physical or mental activity. Action verbs can be divided into two kinds, depending on whether they take a direct object or not.

Transitive verbs are verbs which **take a direct object**. You can see the word *transit* in the name, which is related to *transport*. Think of a truck or transit vehicle delivering something. The transitive verb *transports* the action of the verb to the direct object.

> subject ⟶ transitive verb ⟶ direct object
>
> *(I'm transporting a delivery!)*

Offer is an example of a **transitive** verb. It requires a direct object:

> *I offered lunch.*   *I offered my book.*   *I offered to help with the project.*

Sure, you can just say, "*I offer,*" but your listener will probably think, "*Offer* **what**?" They will be looking for the direct object, the answer to their question. Transitive verbs must have direct objects to make sense.

Intransitive verbs never take a direct object. In fact, you can't use a direct object with one at all! Let's look at the verb **arrive**, an **intransitive** verb. Try filling in a direct object in this sentence:

> *I arrive* _____ .

Anything that fits in the blank that makes sense (like *I arrive soon*) is an adverb, not a direct object. You don't ever **arrive** something; you just **arrive**.

Some verbs can be either transitive or intransitive. Look at the following two examples that both use the verb *eats*:

> He eats lunch.   Eats **what**? Eats **lunch**. **Lunch** is the direct object of **eats**.
> **Eats** is a transitive verb in this sentence.

> He eats quickly.   Eats **what**? There's no answer. *(quickly* answers the question *eats* **how**?)
> **Eats** is an intransitive verb in this sentence.

So why do you need to know all this? Well, there's one more grammar skill that can really make you look sharp, like you really know your stuff, and that's how to know when to use certain commonly confused words.

There are a few very common verbs that we use all the time where knowing transitive/intransitive makes a big difference. Those are **lie/lay**, **sit/set,** and **raise/rise**. Many native English speakers get these confused all the time. In most situations, it might not matter—the listener will probably understand what you mean. But if you're trying to make sure you're precise and accurate, it's important. You already have the skills to know the difference.

Lay/Lie	Present Tense	Past Tense
transitive	lay(s)* The chicken lays the egg. (*Lays what? Lays the egg.* = **transitive**)	laid The chicken laid the egg yesterday. (*Laid what? Laid the egg.* = **transitive**)
intransitive	lie(s) They lie on the grass. (*Lie what? No answer.* = **intransitive**)	lay(s)* They lay on the grass yesterday. (*Lay what? No answer.* = **intransitive**)

*Yikes, the present tense of lay is exactly the same as the past tense of lie! Good thing you know about direct objects!

Raise/Rise	Present Tense	Past Tense
transitive	raise(s) They raise the flag. (*Raise what? Raise the flag.* = **transitive**)	raised They raised the flag yesterday. (*Raised what? Raised the flag.* = **transitive**)
intransitive	rise(s) The sun rises in the morning. (*Rises what? No answer.* = **intransitive**)	rose The sun rose yesterday morning. (*Rose what? No answer.* = **intransitive**)

Set/Sit	Present Tense	Past Tense
transitive	set(s)* She sets the book on the table. (*Sets what? Sets the book.* = **transitive**)	set* She set the book on the table. (*Set what? Set the book.* = **transitive**)
intransitive	sit They sit on the stairs. (*Sit what? No answer.* = **intransitive**)	sat They sat on the stairs. (*Sat what? No answer.* = **intransitive**)

Here's a hint to help you remember: The **intransitive** verbs are all things that you can do as an action with your own body. You lie down, you rise up, you sit down—right? But the **transitive** verbs are all things that you do to something else. You set a book down, you raise a flag, you lay an egg... wait, what? Well, you get the point! The hardest part is keeping them straight in your head, especially because the words all look very similar, and, in fact, are sometimes the same! Remember that you can always look at these notes for help to know the difference. Or think about other ways to help you remember—can you draw some silly pictures of the actions to help?

16 EXERCISE A

Transitive and Intransitive Verbs: Exercise A

Directions
Circle the correct word to complete each sentence.

1) I love to talk to Grandma about her childhood on the farm as she (**sits**, sets) on the porch.

2) Even before the sun (raised, **rose**), she and her brothers were up to do their chores.

3) One of her jobs was to pick up the hens' eggs every morning and carefully (**lay**, lie) them in her basket.

   Hint: Think about **when** this action is happening. What tense is the verb? Then ask the question to find out if there is a direct object: verb **what**? Use the chart for this one!

4) Her father had twelve hens contentedly (**sitting**, setting) on their nests.

5) Some days the hens would (lie, **lay**) one egg each!

Directions
Mark the errors in the following sentences using the editing marks you have learned. There are seven errors. If you need to change one word to another to correct any errors, cross it out and write the correct word above.

6) "After I picked up the eggs," said Grandma, "I'd take them into the house so Ma could make breakfast. We took what we needed for breakfast, and anything left over would be taken to Mr. Taylor's store in the town to sell. As a matter of fact, it was my job to take the eggs into town to Mr. Taylor every day. Ma and I would use our egg money to buy ribbons, candy, and other little extra treats. Yes, I have many good memories about Ma and me and that egg money!"

Exercise A 16

Directions

In each sentence below there is a comma split. All of the commas in each sentence and the lines below them are numbered. Identify the comma split and write its number in the space next to the sentence number. On the lines under each, write what the comma is splitting on the appropriate line. On the other lines, write the "buzzword" for that punctuation rule. Remember that each pair of quotation marks only counts as one thing. There is a number under the open quote mark or the entire title, but there is not one under the close quote mark.

__1__ 7) My great-grandfather was, a sergeant in the US Marine Corps during World War II, and he
                                                             1   2   3

had a flagpole in the yard.

    #1 _splits linking verb and complement_

    #2 _capitalize_

    #3 _compound sentence_

__2__ 8) My great-uncle Tom's job, was to raise the flag and play "America the Beautiful" on his bugle!
                          1 2   3

    #1 _possessives_

    #2 _splits subject and verb_

    #3 _titles_

__1__ 9) Everybody in the family knew their job and did it every, morning in this busy,
                                                                              1   2

energetic family.

    #1 _splits noun and adjective_

    #2 _two adjectives tests_

16 EXERCISE B

Transitive and Intransitive Verbs: Exercise B

Directions
Circle the correct word to complete each sentence.

1) One of Grandma's jobs was to (sit, (set)) the table before meals.

2) She would carefully (lie, (lay)) the forks, knives, and spoons at each place.

3) Her mother was determined to (rise, (raise)) her children with good table manners.

4) After the family ((sat), set) down at the table, they would say grace.

5) After lunch, her mother would ((lie), lay) down with the baby while Grandma did the dishes.

Directions
Mark the errors in the following sentences using the editing marks you have learned. There are seven errors. If you need to change one word to another to correct any errors, cross it out and write the correct word above.

6) Grandma has two brothers named tom and Edward. Tom is the eldest of all of the children, and he took over the farm after his father passed away. He was an expert on farm management, and he wrote a book on it called Anybody Can Manage a Farm. Uncle Tom's book was published on June 3, 1967, and the whole family was extremely proud. I once visited Great-Uncle Tom on the farm, and I noticed that he always maintained his equipment perfect*ly*. He said that was one of the most important things about being a successful farmer.

Exercise B 16

Directions

In each sentence below there is a comma split. All of the commas in each sentence and the lines below them are numbered. Identify the comma split and write its number in the space next to the sentence number. On the lines under each, write what the comma is splitting on the appropriate line. On the other lines, write the "buzzword" for that punctuation rule. Remember that each pair of quotation marks only counts as one thing. There is a number under the open quote mark or the entire title, but there is not one under the close quote mark.

_3_ 7) After lunch in the afternoon, Grandma would lie down for a while, and that was when we
                                     1   2
    had many little, talks.
                    3

   #1 _introductory element_

   #2 _transitive/intransitive verb_

   #3 _splits noun and adjective_

_3_ 8) "Maddie, you're my favorite grandchild, but I, shouldn't say so," she said one day.
        1   2   3

   #1 _quotation marks_

   #2 _direct addres_

   #3 _splits subject and verb_

_1_ 9) One day she gave me, her mother's locket and told me it was a special gift between her and me.
                           1   2   3

   #1 _splits indirect object and direct object_

   #2 _possessives_

   #3 _which pronoun?_

16 EXERCISE C

Transitive and Intransitive Verbs: Exercise C

Directions
Circle the correct word to complete each sentence.

1) After Grandma gave me the locket, I (sat, (set)) it carefully on my chest of drawers.

2) I opened my jewelry box and (lay, (laid)) the locket carefully in it.

3) My mom ((raised), rose) me to be careful about family heirlooms like the locket.

4) That night when I ((lay), laid) on my bed, I thought about Grandma's stories.

5) When I am an old lady, I'll ((sit), set) on the porch and tell them to my grandchildren!

Directions
Mark the errors in the following sentences using the editing marks you have learned. There are seven errors. If you need to change one word to another to correct any errors, cross it out and write the correct word above.

6) Once a year, Grandma and her family always went to the state fair. One year her father took the family's prized hog, and he fully expected to get a blue ribbon for that hog! Well, the hog was so enormous they almost couldn't get him into the truck. The hog, as a matter of fact, wasn't at all interested in climbing up the ramp into the bed of the truck. "Edward, go into the kitchen and get that peach cobbler I baked for Mrs. Cramer," said Great-Grandma. Uncle Edward grabbed the peach cobbler, climbed into the bed of the truck, and that old hog went racing up the ramp!

EXERCISE C **16**

Directions
In each sentence below there is a comma split. All of the commas in each sentence and the lines below them are numbered. Identify the comma split and write its number in the space next to the sentence number. On the lines under each, write what the comma is splitting on the appropriate line. On the other lines, write the "buzzword" for that punctuation rule. Remember that each pair of quotation marks only counts as one thing. There is a number under the open quote mark or the entire title, but there is not one under the close quote mark.

_3_ 7) The hog's name was Baxter, and Uncle Edward hurled, that cobbler at him, yelling, "Baxter,
            1   2   3

slow down!"

#1 _possessives_

#2 _compound sentence_

#3 _splits verb and direct object_

_3_ 8) At the sight of that cobbler, it was clear that Baxter had no, idea of slowing down.
                        1   2   3

#1 _introductory element_

#2 _capitalize_

#3 _splits noun and adjective_

_1_ 9) Uncle Edward, took one look at Baxter, turned as white as a sheet, and vaulted over the side
                    1   2

of the truck like an Olympic gymnast!
                    3

#1 _splits subject and verb_

#2 _items in a series_

#3 _capitalize_

16 ASSESSMENT

Transitive and Intransitive Verbs: Assessment

Directions
Circle the correct word to complete each sentence.

Each correctly chosen word is worth one point.

1) After he got into the truck and ate all the peach cobbler, Baxter (**lay**, laid) down quietly for the rest of the trip.

2) Great-Grandma (sat, **set**) her prize peach preserves on the seat next to her.

3) Hope (raised, **rose**) up in her heart when she thought about winning a blue ribbon for them.

4) She and Great-Grandpa had (sat, **set**) their hopes on winning.

5) When the truck went over a bump, Great-Grandma picked up her preserves and then carefully (lay, **laid**) them on her lap for the rest of the trip.

___
5

Directions
Mark the errors in the following sentences using the editing marks you have learned. There are seven errors. If you need to change one word to another to correct any errors, cross it out and write the correct word above.

Each corrected error is worth one point.

6) "We knew we were at the fair when we could hear, the music coming from the carnival" Grandma said. "I was so, excited that I was going to spend the entire day enjoying myself! The sounds, the sights, and the smells were just wonderful. Ma and Papa gave us kids a little money to spend at the midway. By noon, however, we had to find Baxters pen to see our enormous, beautiful hog as he ~~laid~~ *lay* in his straw."

___
7

ASSESSMENT 16

Directions

In each sentence below there is a comma split. All of the commas in each sentence and the lines below them are numbered. Identify the comma split and write its number in the space next to the sentence number. On the lines under each, write what the comma is splitting on the appropriate line. On the other lines, write the "buzzword" for that punctuation rule. Remember that each pair of quotation marks only counts as one thing. There is a number under the open quote mark or the entire title, but there is not one under the close quote mark.

Identifying the comma split is worth two points. Identifying what is split and which buzzwords apply is worth one point each.

$\frac{3}{2}$ 7) Mr. Hiram Hooker was the head of the judging committee, and he, looked Baxter over
                                                    1   2   3

from head to tail.

    $\frac{}{1}$ #1 *capitalize*
    $\frac{}{1}$ #2 *compound sentence*
    $\frac{}{1}$ #3 *splits subject and verb*

$\frac{3}{2}$ 8) After a brief conference with the committee, he announced, "Baxter wins, first prize!"
                                                            1   2   3

    $\frac{}{1}$ #1 *introductory element*
    $\frac{}{1}$ #2 *gear change comma*
    $\frac{}{1}$ #3 *splits verb and direct object*

$\frac{1}{2}$ 9) Papa, Tom, Ed, and I, went to find Ma," said Grandma, "and she was standing there
                                         1   2

with her preserves, a big smile, and the blue ribbon!"
                             3

    $\frac{}{1}$ #1 *splits subject and verb*
    $\frac{}{1}$ #2 *quotation marks*
    $\frac{}{1}$ #3 *items in a series*

$\frac{}{15}$

$\frac{}{27}$ Total Points $\frac{22}{27} = 80\%$

Bibliography

Florey, Kitty Burns. Sister Bernadette's Barking Dog: The Quirky History and Lost Art of Diagramming Sentences. Orlando, FL: Harcourt, 2007.

Garner, Bryan A. Garner's Modern English Usage. Oxford: Oxford University Press, 2016.

Garner, Bryan A. The Chicago Guide to Grammar, Usage, and Punctuation. Chicago, IL: The University of Chicago Press, 2016.

Truss, Lynne. Eats, Shoots & Leaves: The Zero Tolerance Approach to Punctuation. London: Fourth Estate, 2009.